CONCEPT ART
IDEA BOOK 2

WRITTEN AND ILLUSTRATED
BY JEFFREY HUNT

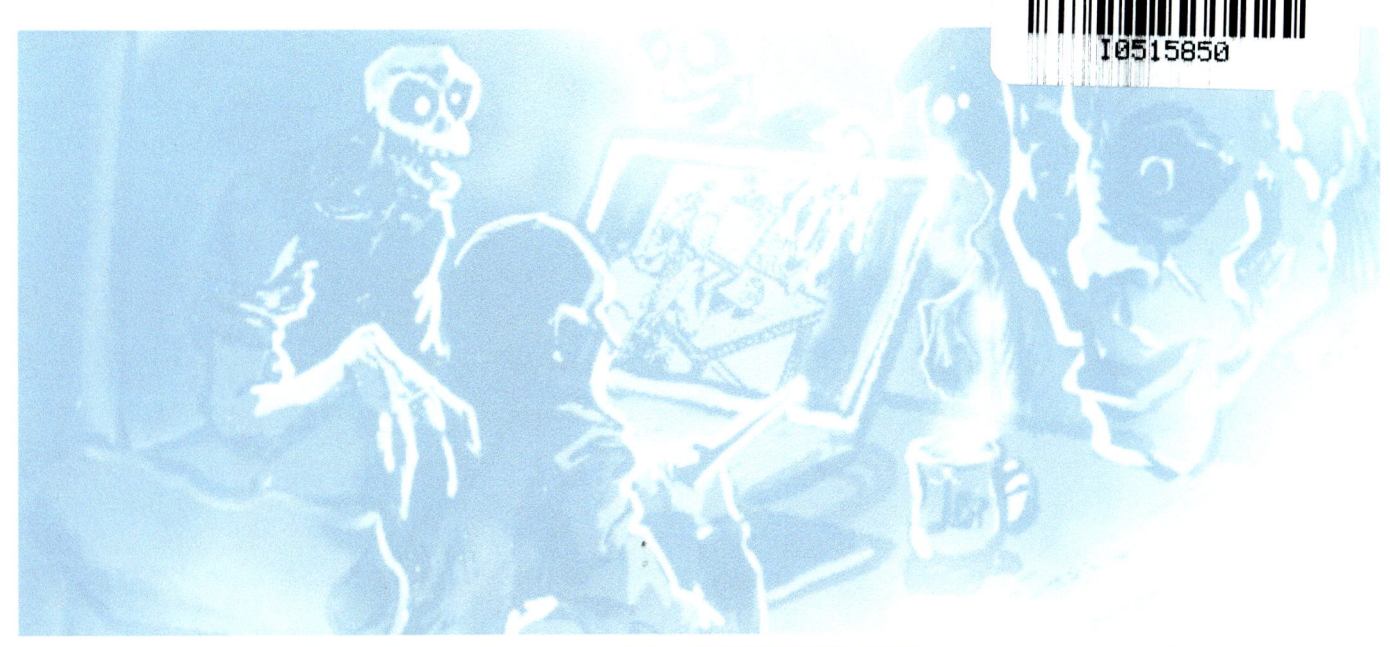

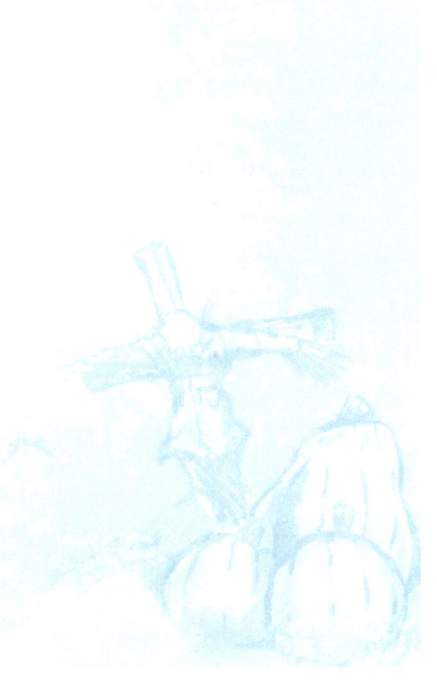

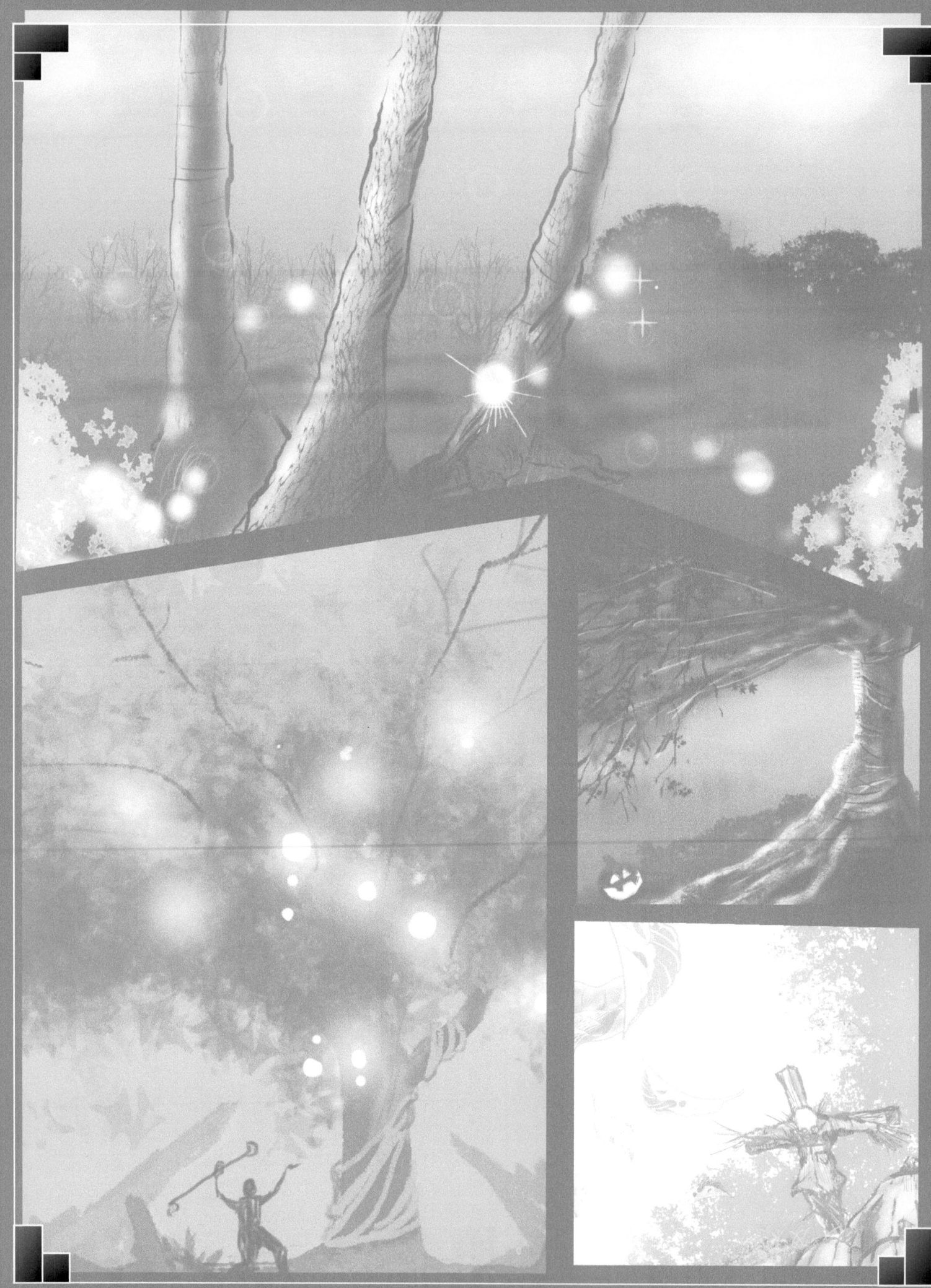

INSIDE THIS BOOK

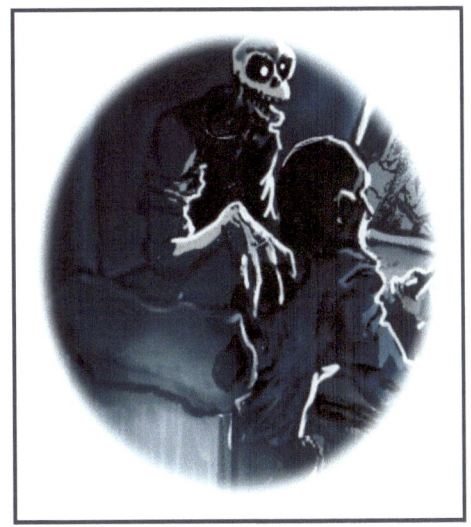

Page 7

Telling My Ideas to Wait in Line

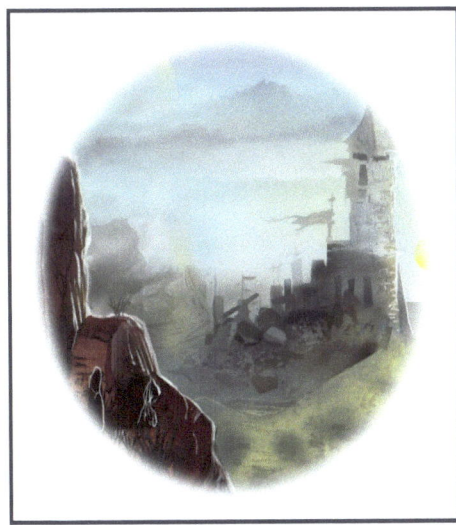

Page 13

Landscapes

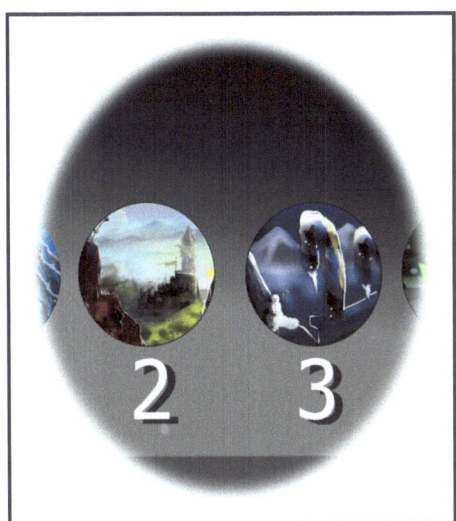

Page 31

Logos

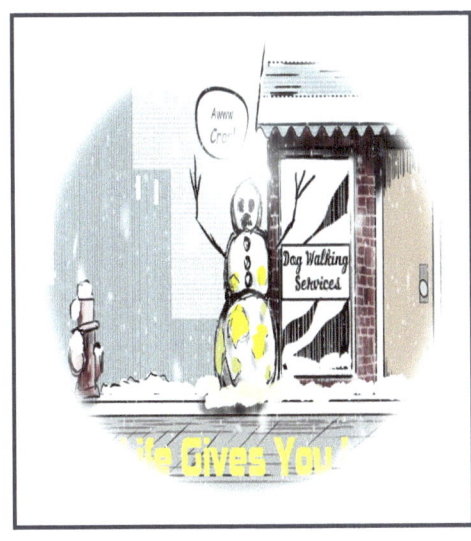

Page 34

When Life Gives You Lemons (Snowman Humor)

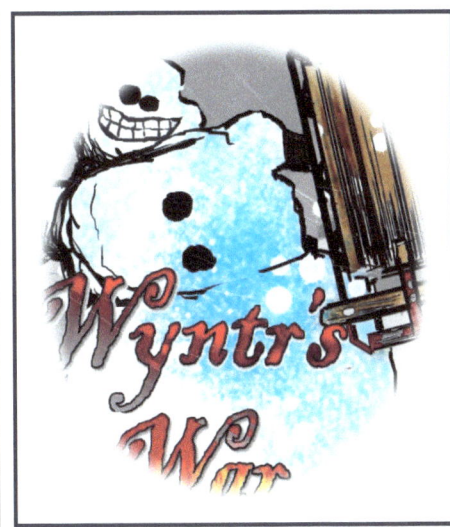

Page 39

Character Design

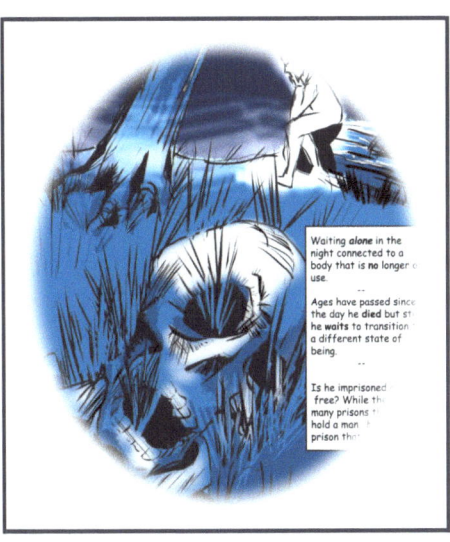

Page 49

Comic Book Art

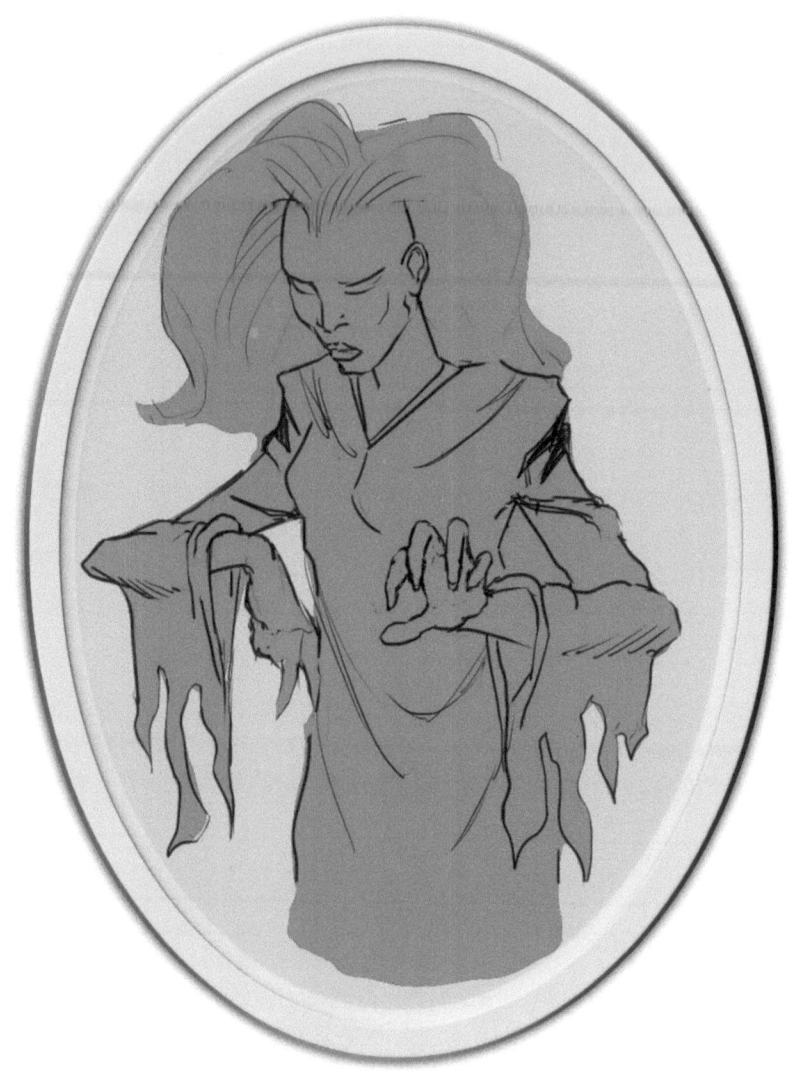

Copyright © 2022 Jeffrey Hunt.

All rights reserved. This book or any portion thereof may not be reproduced or used in any manner whatsoever without the express written permission of the publisher except for the use of brief quotations in a book review.

https://www.artofjeffreyhunt.com

ARTIST STATEMENT

JEFFREY HUNT, FANTASY DIGITAL ARTIST

The Concept Art Idea Book 2 is designed to share my completed works and share a little bit about myself and my processes.

I am mainly a self taught artist but have been creating art since I could hold a pencil. I am an active duty Soldier in the United States Army and strive to improve my art every single day.

As many artists struggle with drawing blocks or just need a little inspiration, it is my hope that those who read this book will find some fuel to get the ideas flowing again.

I am very grateful to all of the artists out there who take time to produce vides on YouTube, write and illustrate e-books, and answer questions. The digital world in which we live makes it easier for anyone who desires to learn to be an artist no matter the skill level. All it really takes is a desire to learn and the fortitude to weather the storm when it gets hard.

Always follow your dreams.

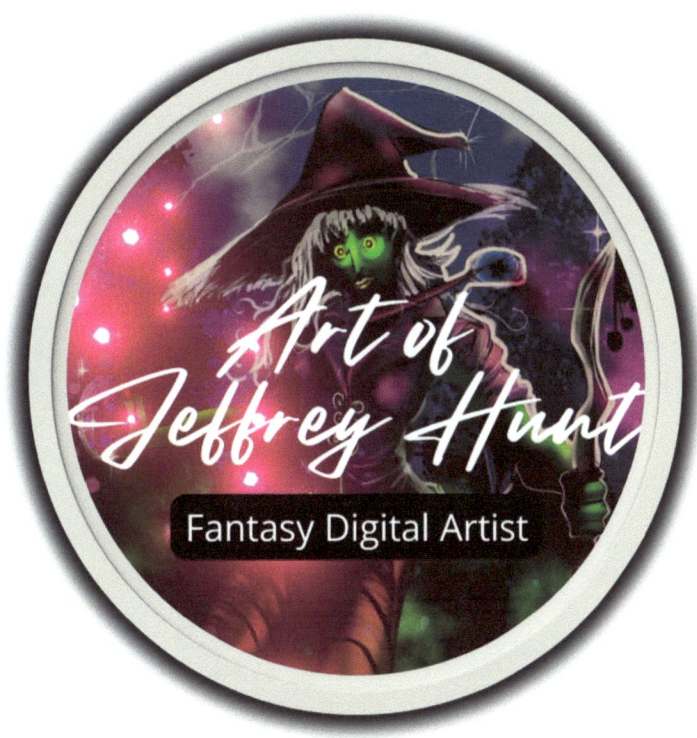

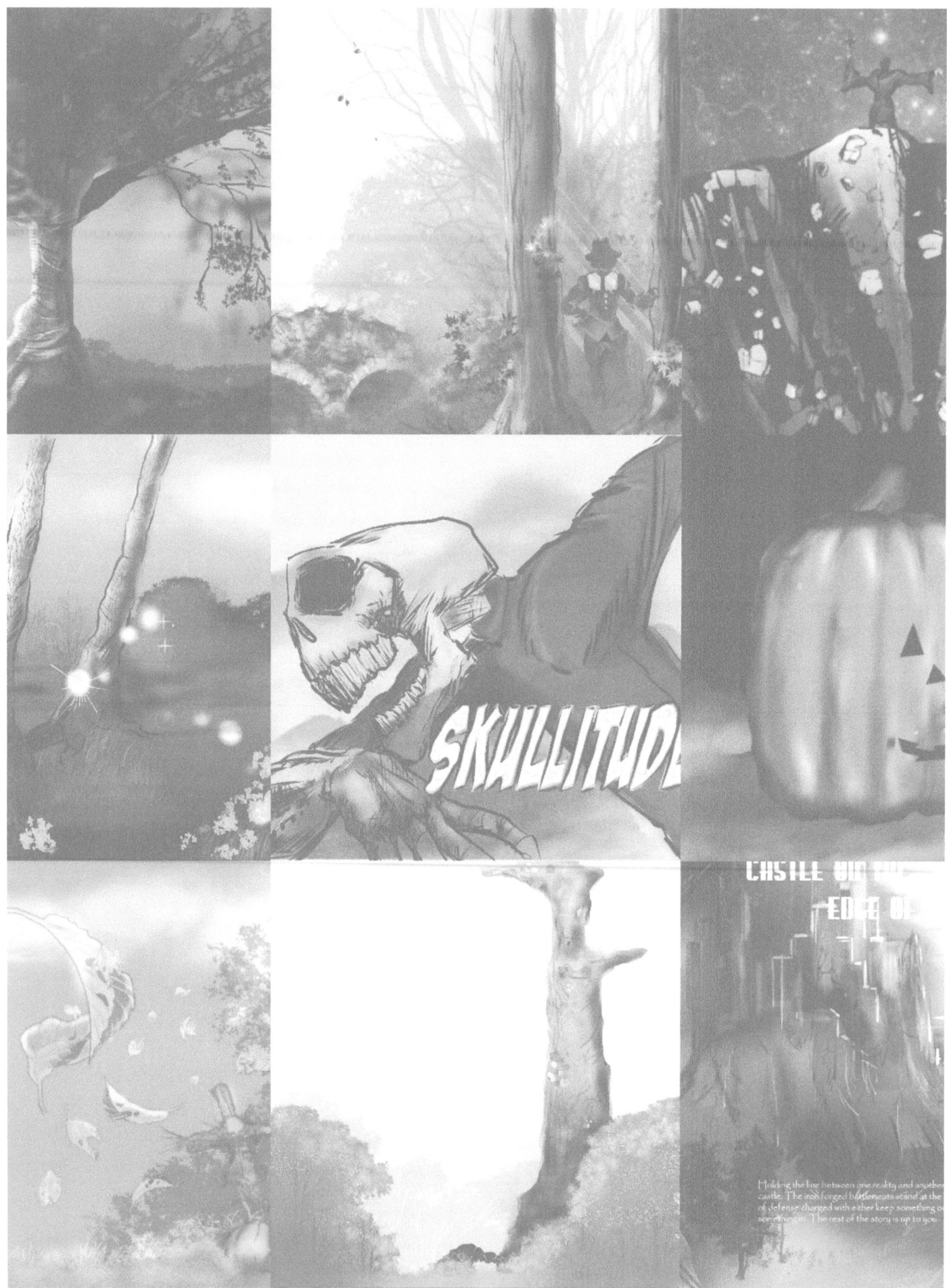

Telling My Ideas to Wait in Line

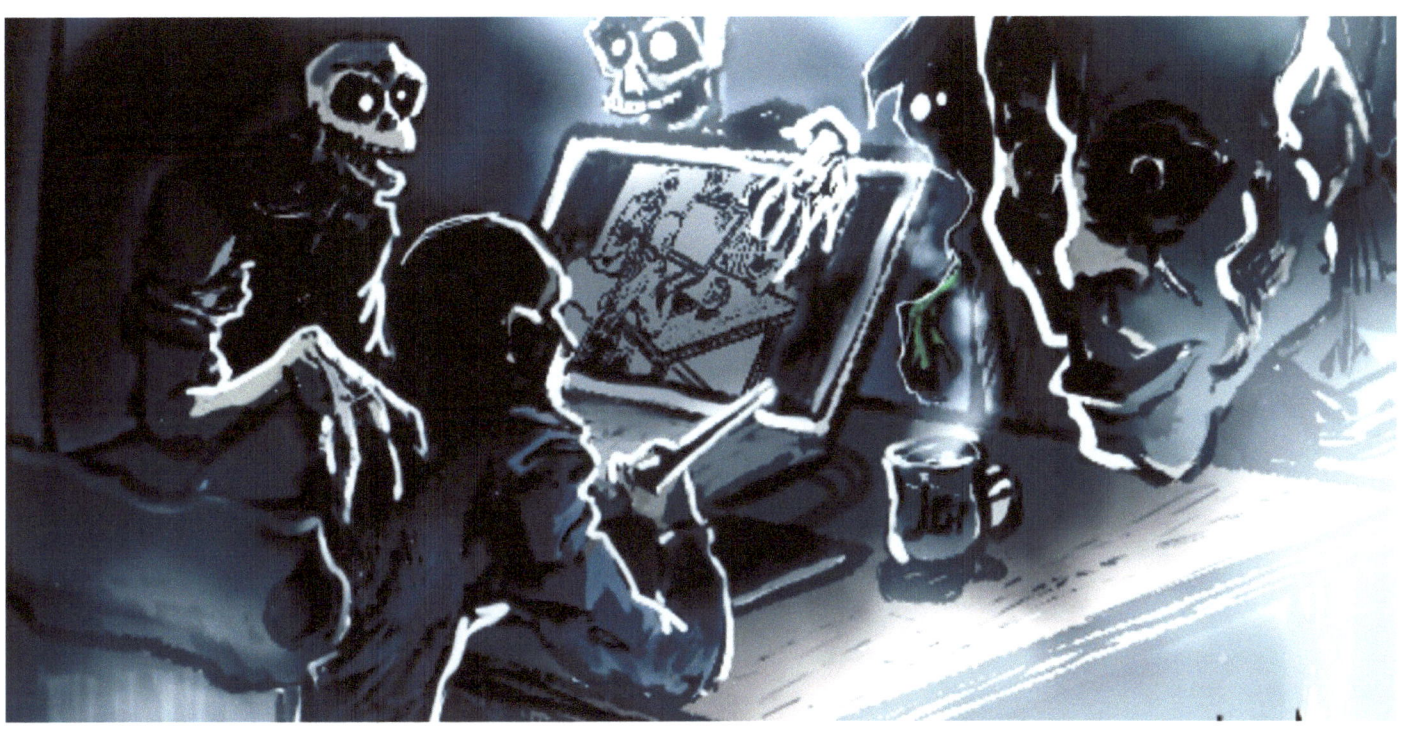

This year I have a lot of ideas for things I want to do and characters I want to create. Sometimes there are so many that they don't want to wait in line at all. It's like they are telling me what I'm going to do next and I have to remind myself that I'm the boss. Much of this just comes from impatience and the need to work on more than one project at once. It just seems like one project eventually competes with the other. Can anyone else relate?

The key to all of this is a carefully planned out year and the self acknowledgement that it's OK not to have to do everything at once. Once I come to grip with that, it makes it much easier to sit back and enjoy the process of just creating art while entertaining others.

I am currently a full time Soldier in the United States Army, raising a family, and producing digital art on the side all while studying art. As I type this, I suddenly feel overwhelmed but I have a lot of support from my family to follow my dreams and that is what matters most.

Every so often the daydreamer in me causes me to lose interest in one project and jump into another. I think that is how I overcome burnout. Having a lot of options gives me the flexibility to choose what I want to work on when I feel stuck on the current project. Sometimes an image might not look right or some element might be throwing off the entire design but the reason eludes me. It's amazing the insight you gain working on a different project and then coming back to the previous one. I think "why didn't I see that error before?"

Creative Process

The banner was specially sized for Facebook. I created a custom template in Clip Studio Paint so that I don't have to recreate the wheel next time that I want to make a another one. Very handy that way. I used almost 20 separate layers all together to get the affects that I was trying for.

Pencils

This was the pencil rough that I started from. Now when I say pencil, I really mean the digital one that I use when I work digitally. I haven't used a regular pencil in a very long time although I do like to doodle still. As you can see, I keep pretty fluid to capture the composition that I want to go for and make sure that if there are any design problems, I can catch it prior to going to far into detail.

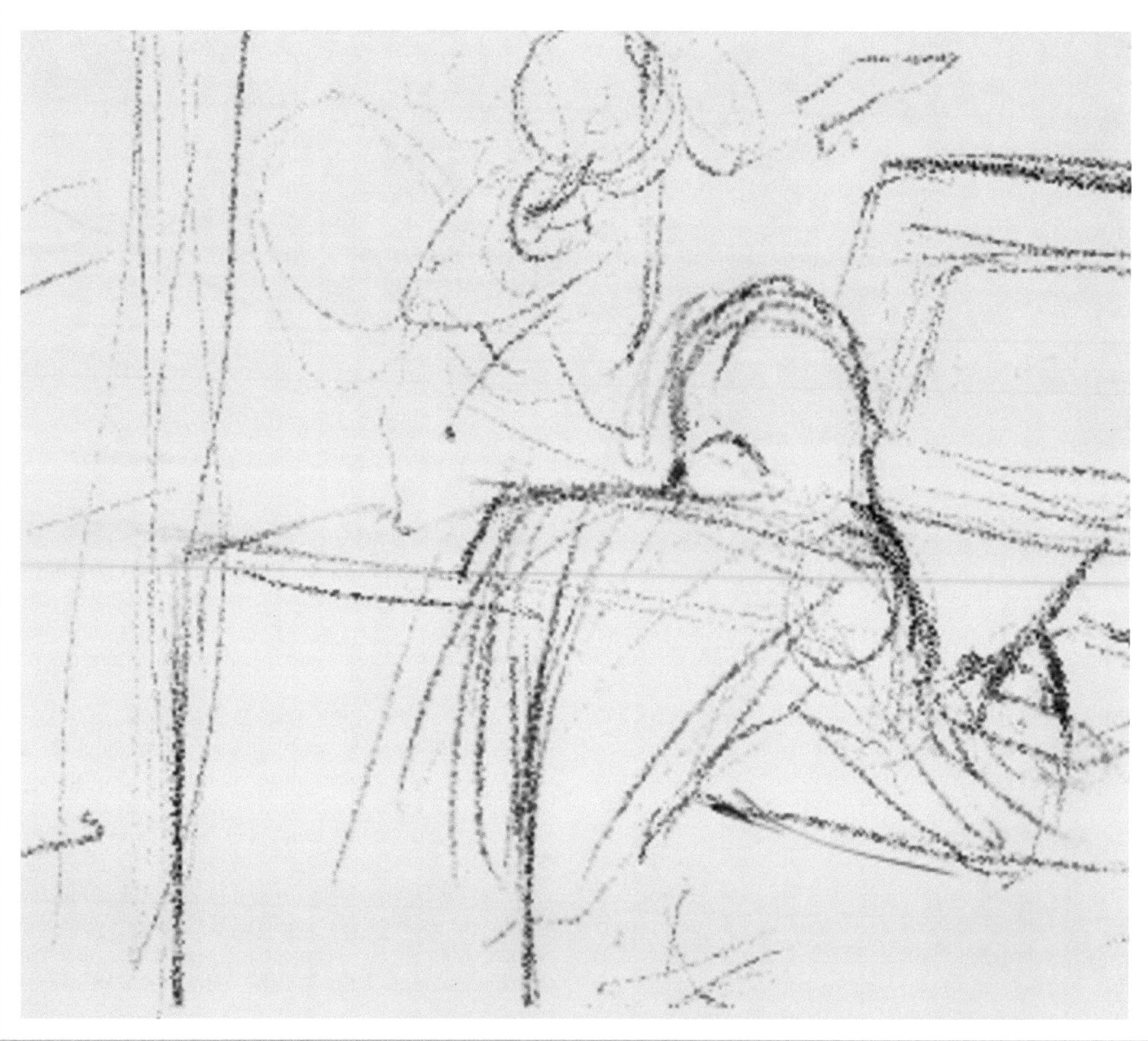

Digital Inks

Depicted below is the digital ink layer over the pencils. During this part I reduce the opacity of the pencils so they don't get in the way. At this point, they are only there for reference so I can keep to the composition that I chose. I also make sure to keep any broken lines out. These are lines that don't connect to another line either due to erasing or not drawing a line far enough over.

If you have broken lines, it makes is more difficult to use color fills during the coloring phase. Alternatively you can manually fill in your colors to makes sure you don't have that problem from the start. There is no one right way to do this though. Each to their own. You can also see that I implied some texture on the table and on the clothes.

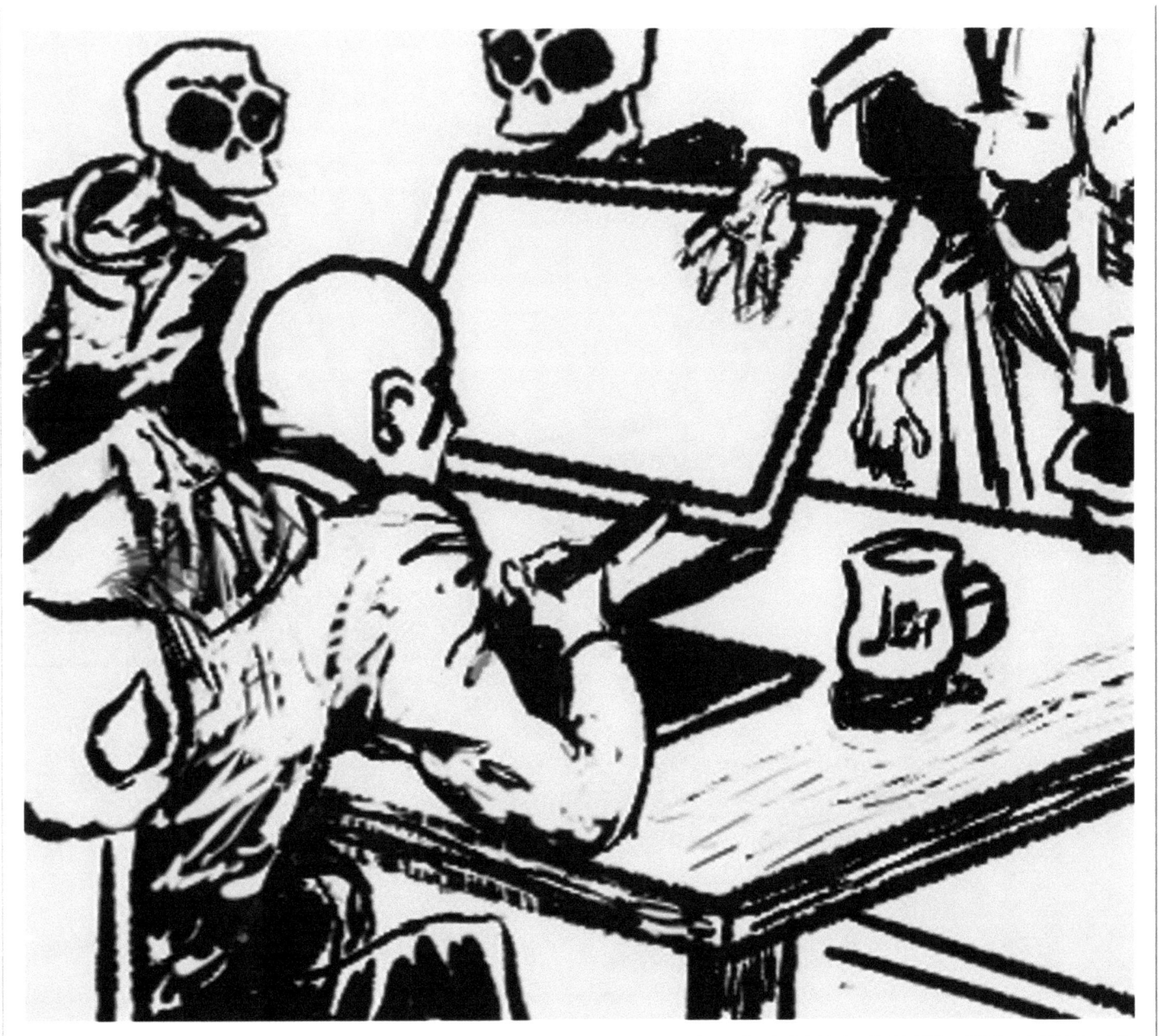

Inked Line art with color flats

Color flats are the base colors that an artist begins with. They can always be changed later but flatting makes it easier to see how well the color choices are working together. During this step, I filled in the colors that I want to start with. You can always change them once you start so it doesn't matter what colors you chose at the start. I knew I wanted to back wall to look smoky or hazy so it just used an air brush. The rest of the colors were used using a bucket tool. This sped up the process quite a bit.

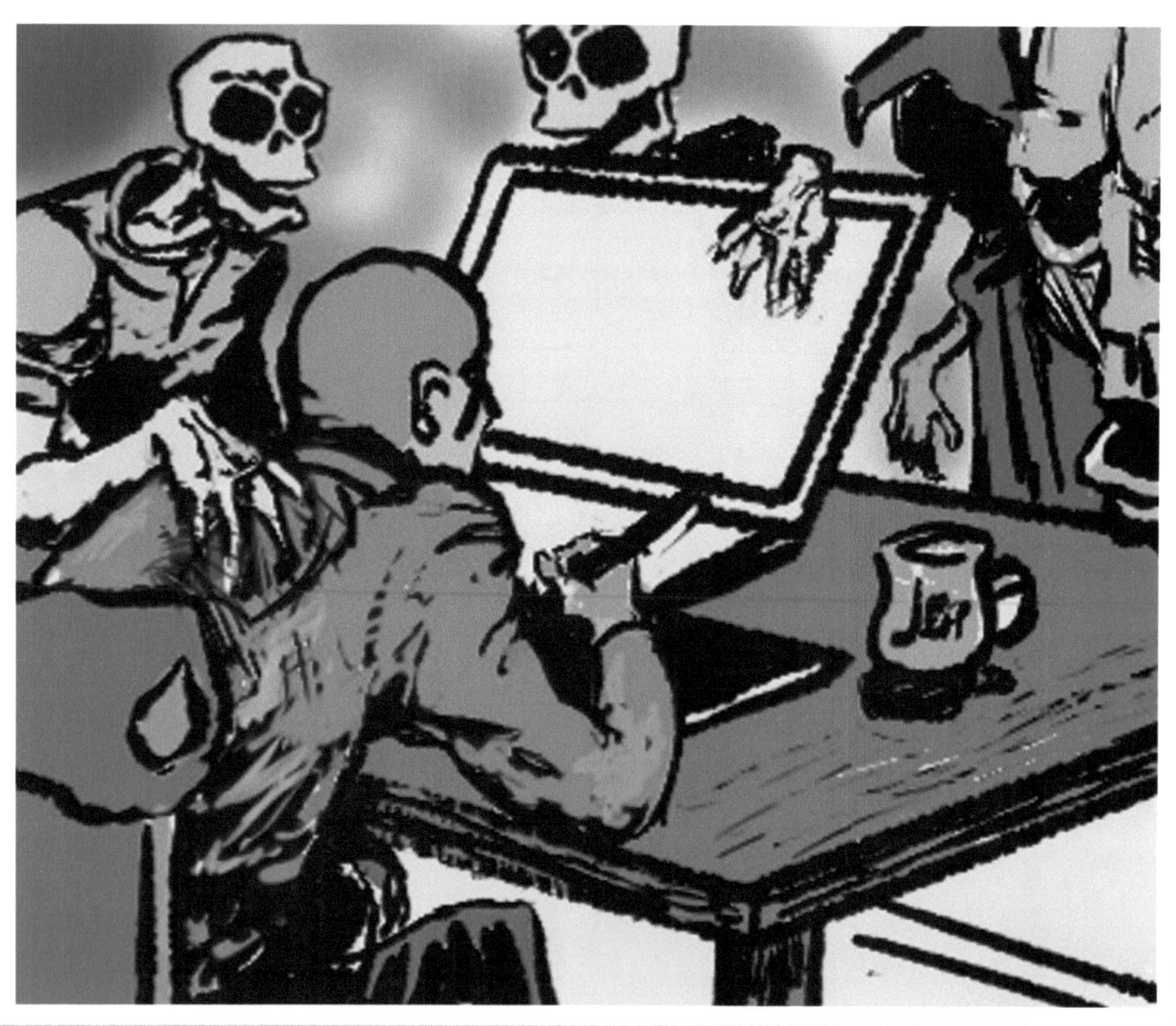

Flats with color shading

This is how I shade and highlight. I use two separate layers for each. The first layer for the highlights is called a screen layer. This allows me to use lighter colors over the darker color and creates a highlight effect. You can also do the same think if you used a Normal Layer just as long as you drop the opacity a bit. A darken layer worked great to get the texture on the chair and clothes more defined. This is a great tool for shading. I hope I'm not losing anyone or getting overly technical. For those who use Photoshop or Clip Studio Paint, you will know what I'm talking about.

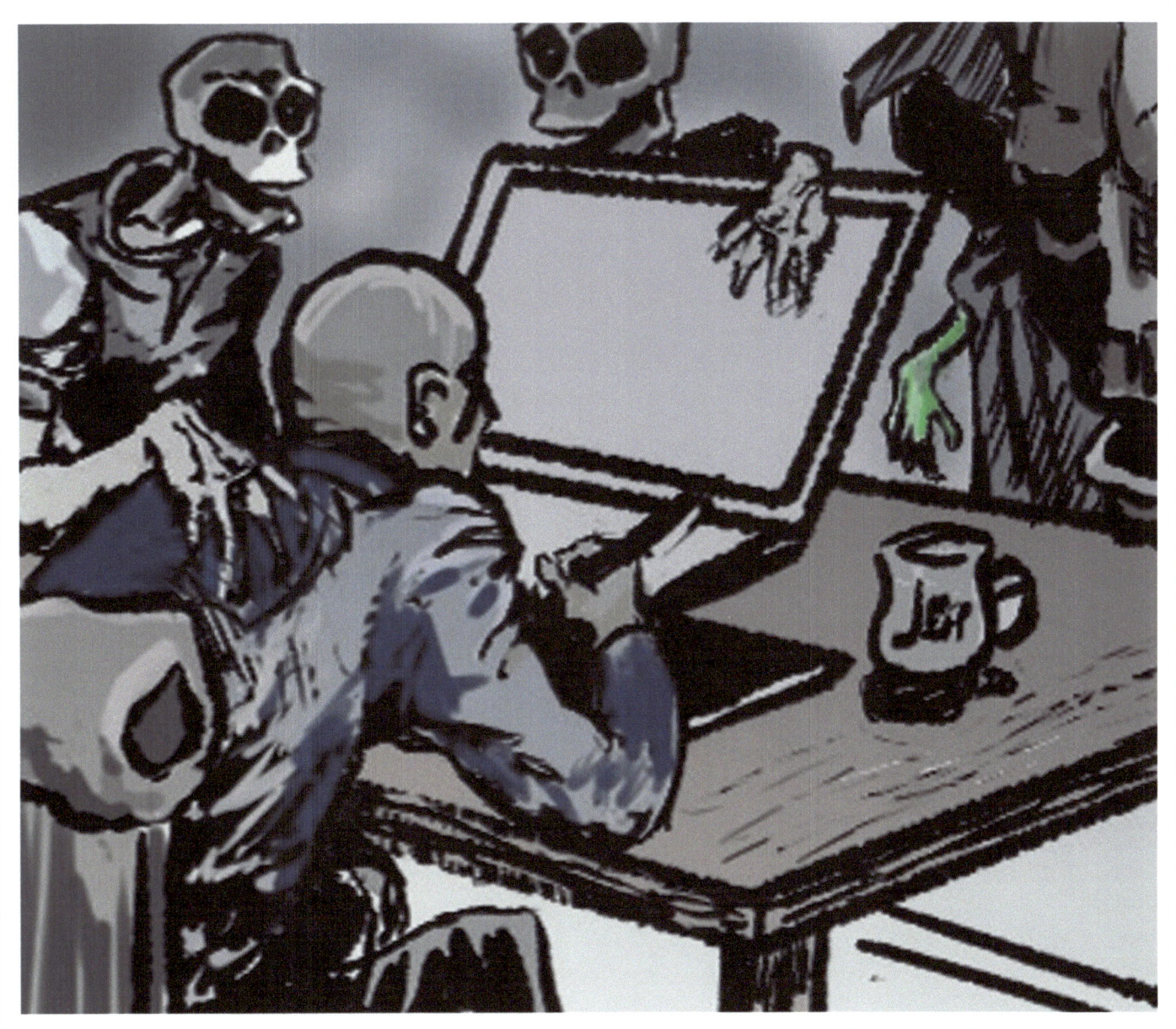

Final Rendering

The final rendering I added a gradient map to give the whole piece a nice unified greenish blue color. This added that extra bit of mood that I was looking for. I also added ambient light shadows along with some finer details during the "polishing" stage. Polishing is basically adding those fine details and correcting any image errors you might find along the way.

If you look close to the image below, the fine white outline pulls the image out away from the background. This is a technique used a lot in comics to separate characters from the background. Lastly, I added a title to the left side using some word art and worked with it until it had a neon style.

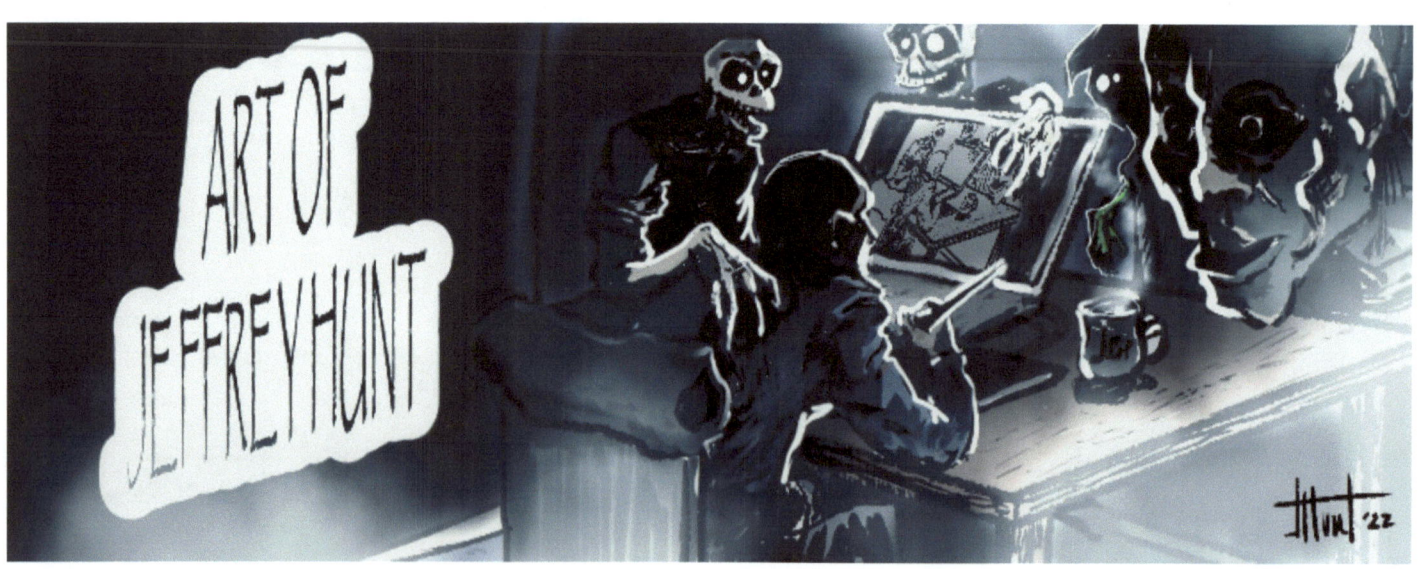

LANDSCAPE CONCEPTS

Landscapes are an awesome way to combine mood enhancing elements with storytelling to create to create an image that really draws the reader into a scene. An artists job is to inspire some type of an emotion into the viewer to ultimately keep them coming back for more.

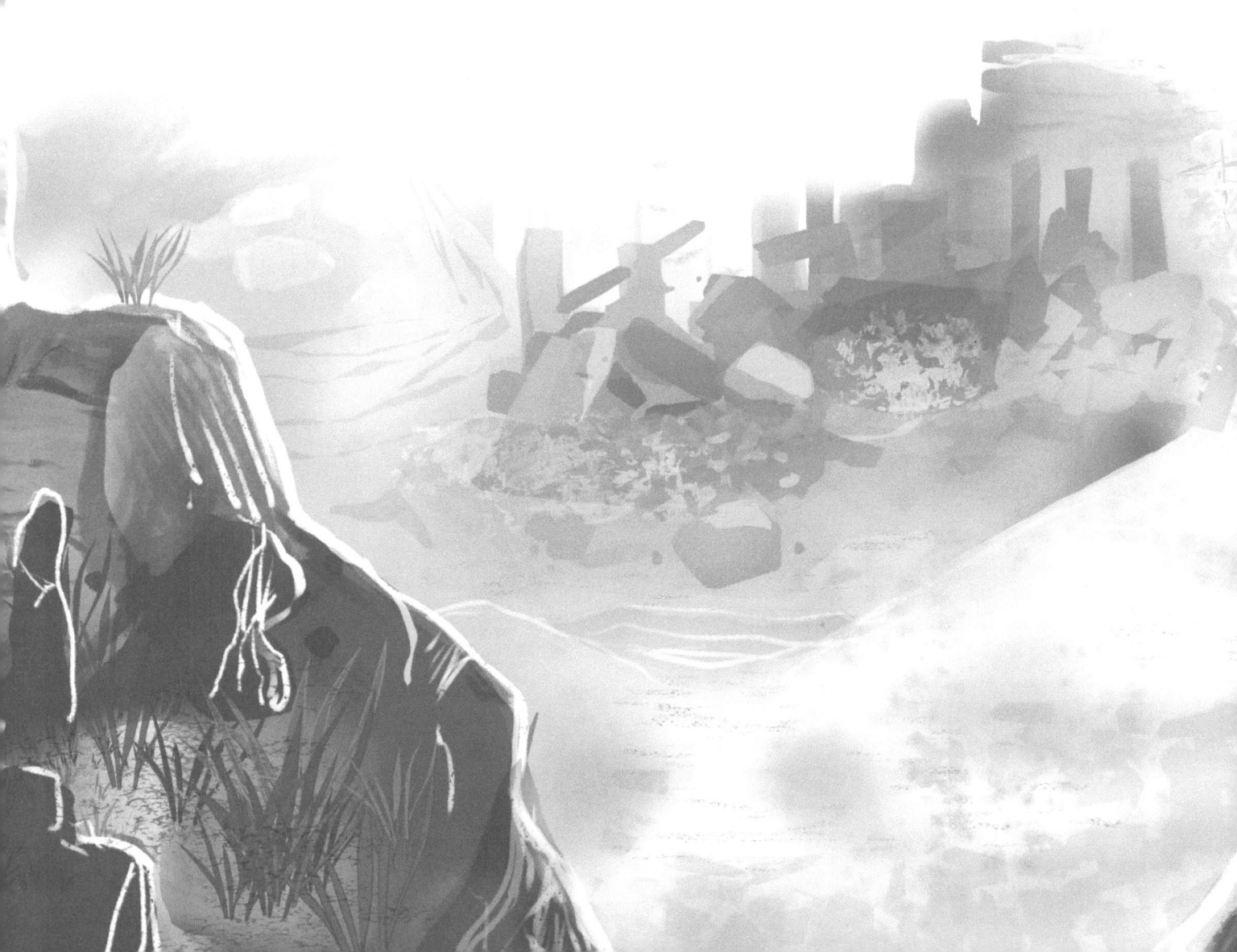

Forgotten Castle

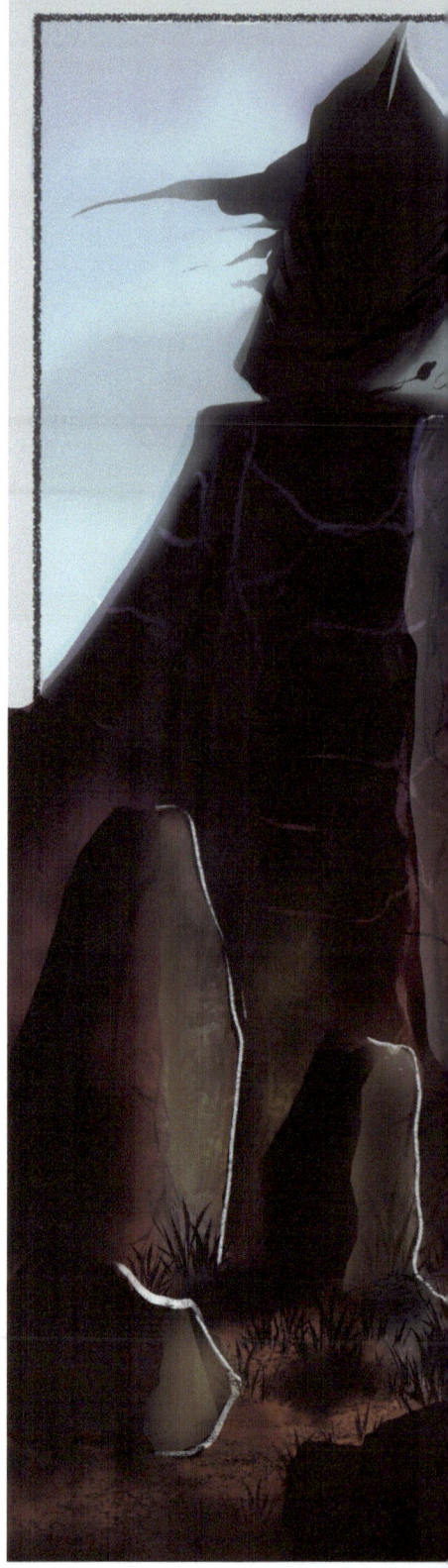

I imagined a tired, weary, traveler overlooking an abandoned castle as if it had once been his home or perhaps waiting for someone once lost to return.

This began as an idea for a book cover. I wanted to convey a large open area with which the viewer could imagine an entire story unfolding. In this case, I imagined a tired, weary, traveler overlooking an abandoned castle as if it had once been his home or perhaps waiting for someone once lost to return. He could even be looking to find lost treasures hidden within.

I designed this using darker shapes in the foreground and less saturated colors in the background to better separate the planes from each other. The lasso tool is a great way to set up the different planes by blocking in the basic shapes. Numerous layers were then used to create atmospheric effects around the sky, the castle, and the ground. There were approximately 30 layers all together.

To separate out the background even more, I used a Hue/Saturation correction layer and painted over the castle area with a light color. I masked out the foreground so only the background would be affected. The lighter color pushed the castle further out of view creating an illusion of depth.

The possibilities are endless with a scene like this. What kind of story would you tell?

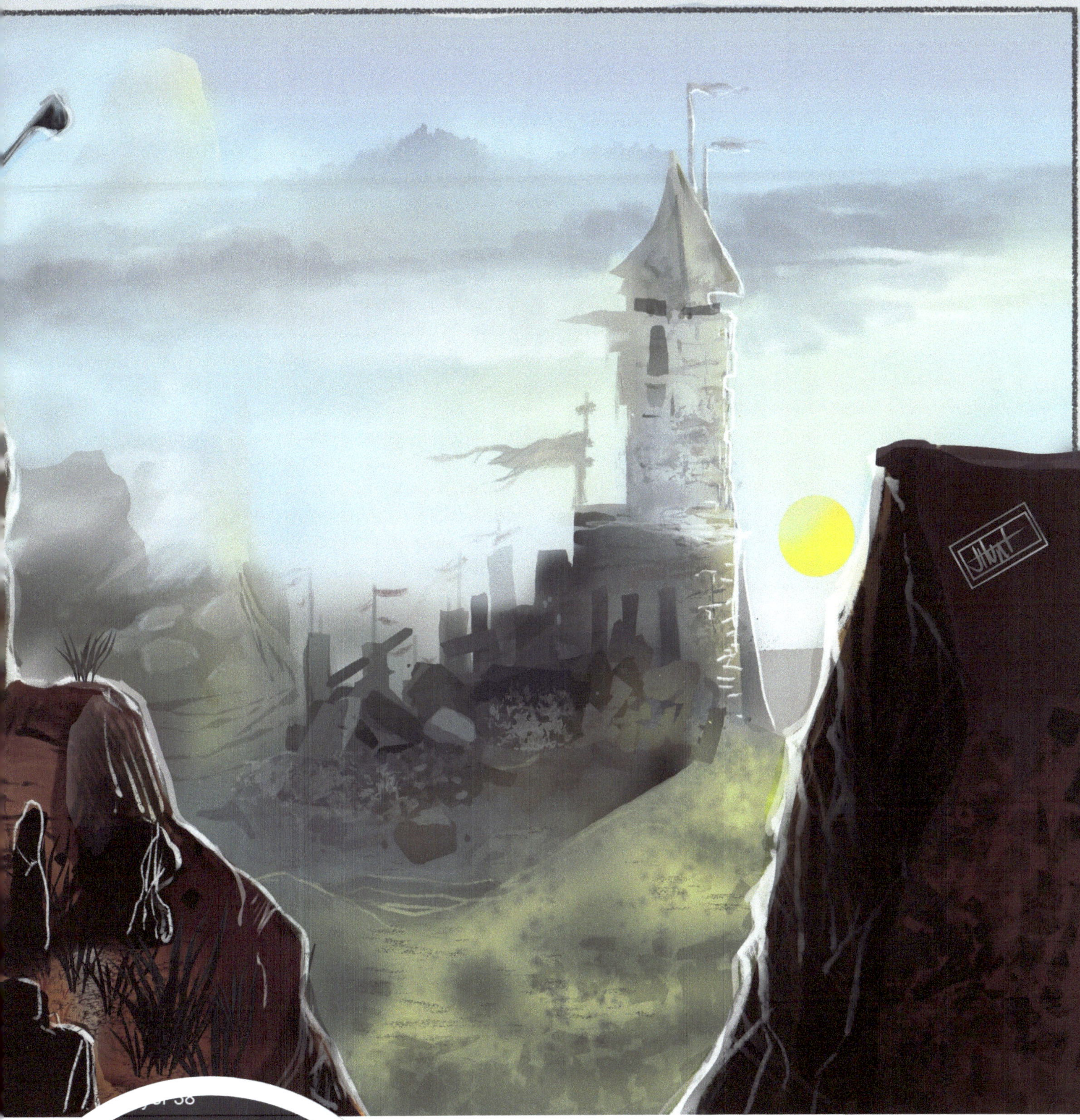

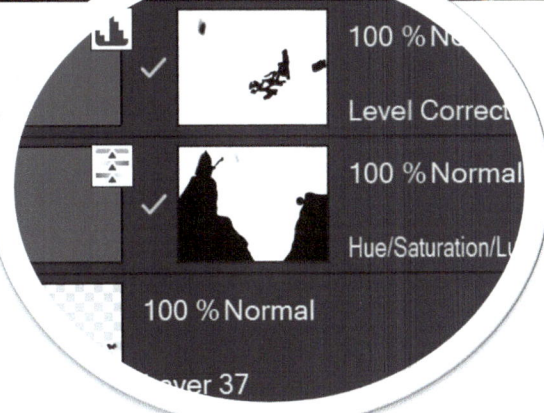

QUICK TIP

Hue/Saturation correction layers make final polishing simple by the power they have to alter or even completely change colors

Winter Cottage

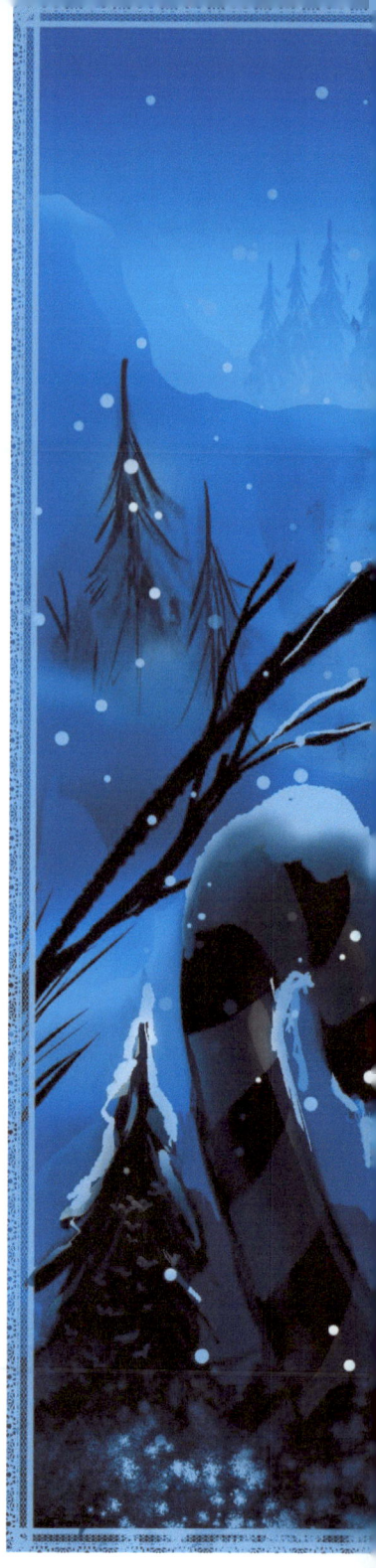

This was the perfect opportunity to use the warm colors of the light to serve as the focal point of the entire scene.

This painting was created during the Christmas holiday and my goal was to design a fantasy winter scene. The cottage is completely buried in snow with the only light coming from the burning candles within the cottage. This was the perfect opportunity to use the warm colors of the light to serve as the focal point of the entire scene. The rest of the scene is dominated by cool colors which progressively get lighter as your eyes go further back. By keeping the color palate a limited to mainly blues, the mood of the scene becomes colder and seemingly more lonely.

I love to use layers to create new and different effects. The candy cane had three layers blended together to combine shadow, surface texture, and volume. The combined effects make the structure look more realistic. I copied and pasted it a few times into the background so that the overall shape language was maintained throughout.

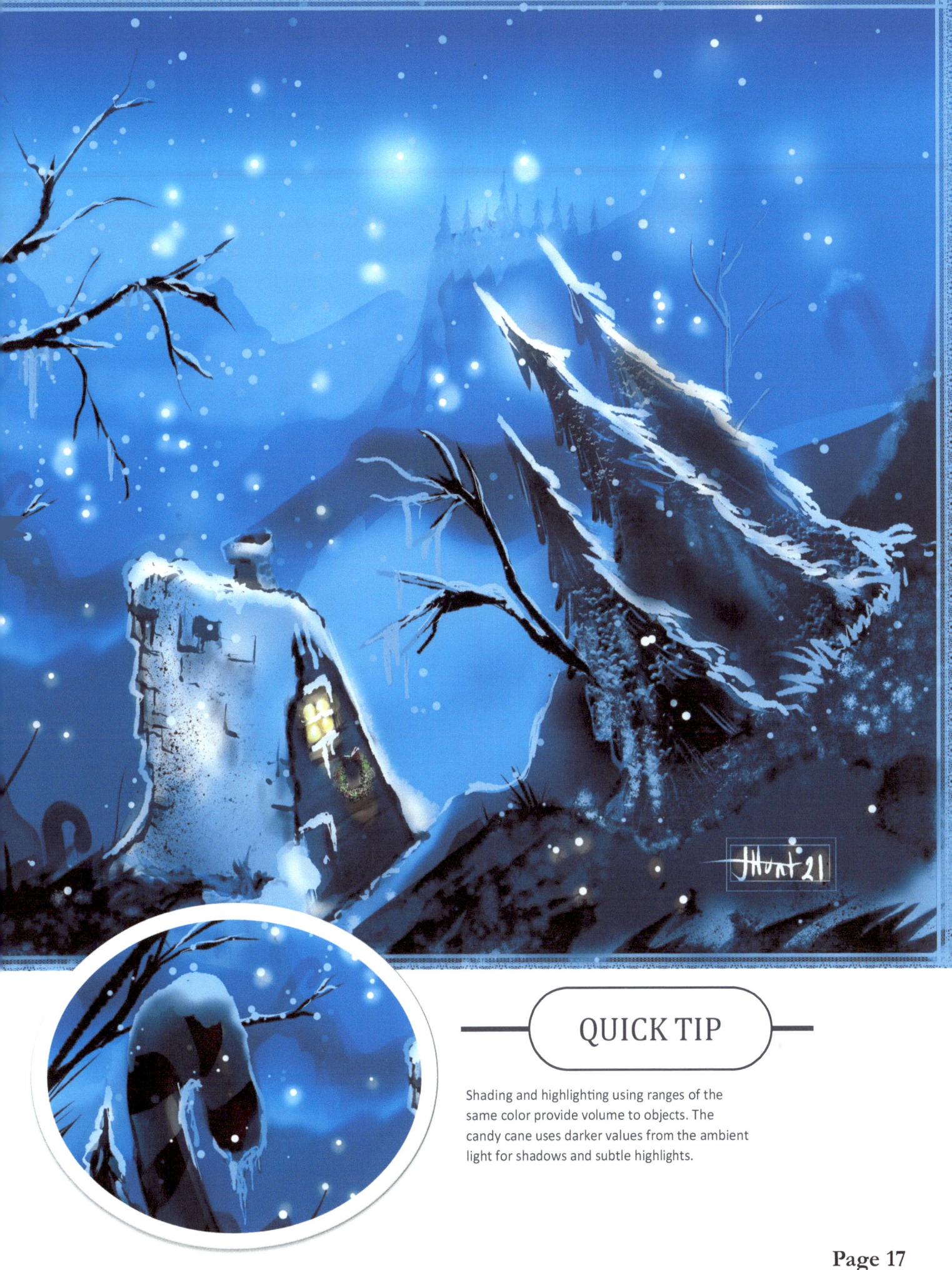

QUICK TIP

Shading and highlighting using ranges of the same color provide volume to objects. The candy cane uses darker values from the ambient light for shadows and subtle highlights.

Page 17

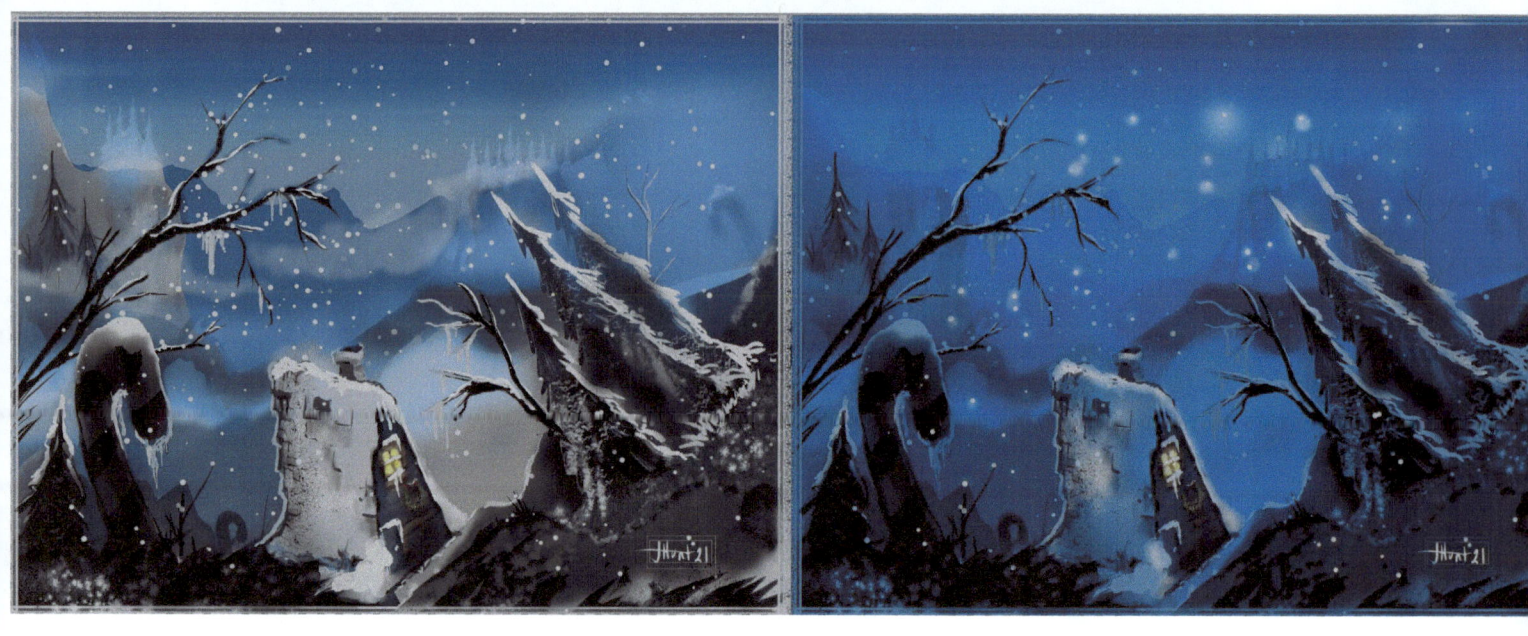

Lighting and Texture

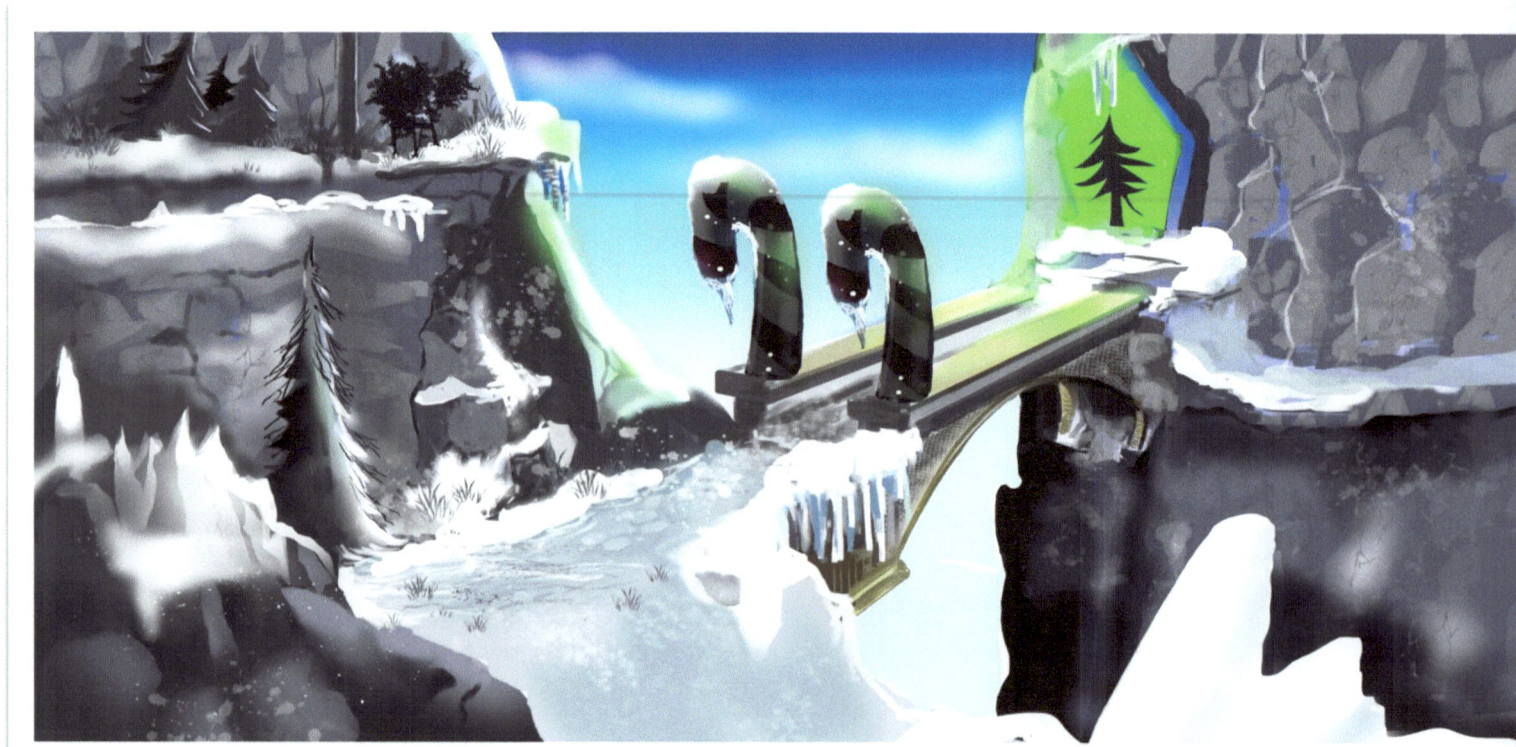

In the example left I have the same painting side by side to show how lighting effects can change the mood of the painting. Using a brightness / contrast adjustment layer, I was able to make the entire scene on the right a lot darker which pulls the warm light out for more of a focal point. The painting bottom left has lots of texture implied on the mountain, the bridge, and the road itself. Detail elements such as this help to create believability and an understanding of the location for the viewer. The smooth texture of the bridge makes it seem more man made.

The Christmas cave painting below is another example of a lighting effect. The gems on the right side were isolated with a separate glow layer to create another ambient light inside of the cave in addition to the light shining off of the ornament. Multiple light sources can bring a special mood to an environment as well as add depth to the characters affected by the light.

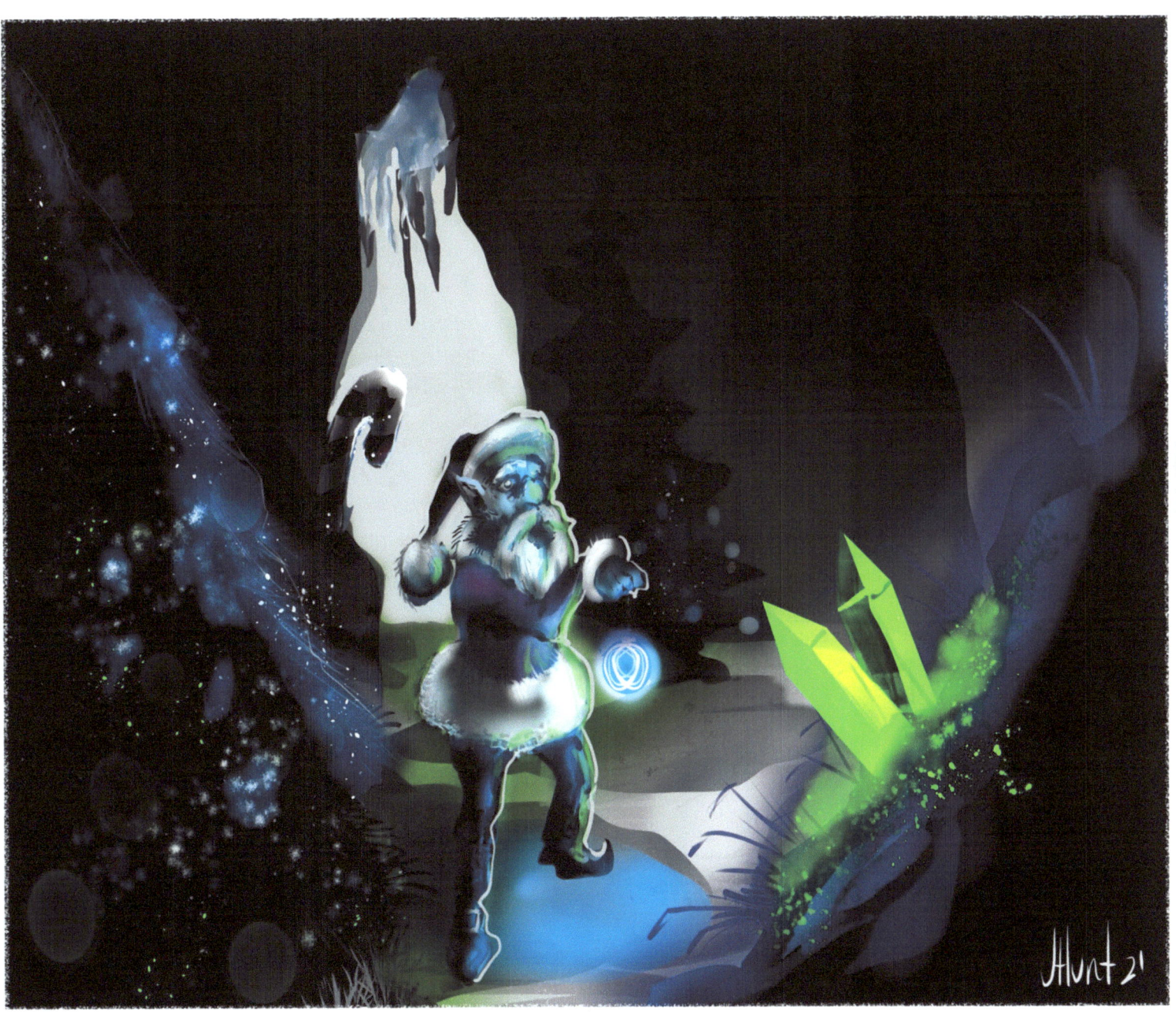

Page 19

THE HALLOWEEN TREE

> *I really wanted the tree to be the most distinct object in the scene other than the pumpkin of course.*

The air is cold and the sky is dimly lit. The colors of orange and yellow dominate the night as they permeate from lit pumpkins and harvest lights. There is a minor wind blowing across your shoulder. It is just enough to make you think a ghost is notifying you of its presence. There are just enough clues to let you know that Summer is gone and won't be returning anytime soon.

The objective of the scene was to capture all of the moody colors of Halloween and accentuate the look of a brightly lit pumpkin by having it reflect off the tree. What do you see?

Five layers were used to create this piece. I used two flat color layers to help pull the tree away from the background of the scene. The tree, inks and colors, are on one layer and the background is on a separate layer. By doing this, I was able to use a blur filter on the background to make it more misty and mysterious without disturbing the look of the tree. I really wanted the tree to be the most distinct object in the scene other than the pumpkin of course.

The glow layer amplified the light from the pumpkin and made it look brighter against the darker background. I didn't put a lot of detail into pumpkin other than the face as a composition strategy to keep the primary focus on the tree.

Instead of using basic flat colors, I used many colored pencils and colored inks to create the color effects that I was seeking. I wanted the scene to look more of a painting than a regular digital image.

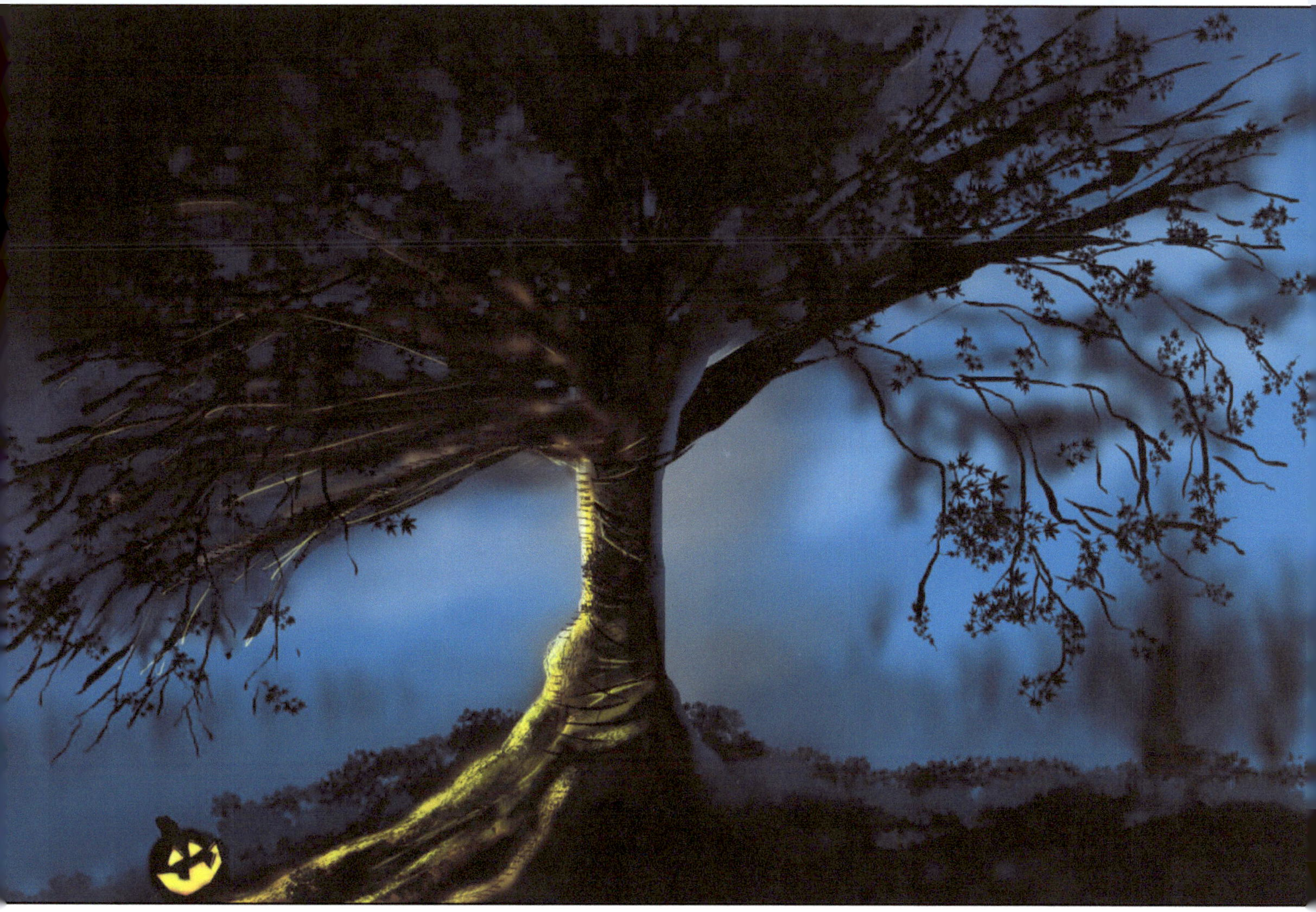

QUICK TIP

Tree texture was simulated using light and shadow with some extra detail pencil lines extruding the wood of the tree out further.

QUICK TIP

The pumpkin light affect was designed by placing the outline of the pumpkin above the glow layer with the bright orange light.

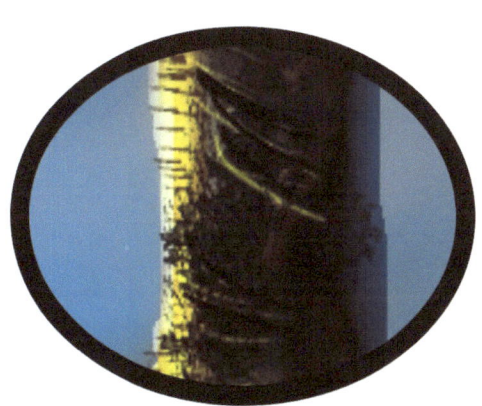

Spirit Falls

Some places might allow you to commune with lost relatives while others might keep you connected to the wisdom of the ages. .

This was an earlier painting that I completed when I first started using Clip Studio Paint. I must have had at least four references opened of waterfalls. A water paint brush helped me to blend the foam of the water and pull it downward. I also adjusted the opacity to make it more transparent.

This was inspired by the thought of how many sacred places there are in the world and what they mean to different people. Some places might allow you to commune with lost relatives while others might keep you connected to the wisdom of the ages. I thought a waterfall might be a neat way to create some connection between man and nature while also capturing a mystical aspect to it.

I think the ghostly lines moving from left to right give the eye some movement as the "spirits" seem to flow in and out of the painting. The bright white of the water against the darker background helps keep the focal point mainly on the water and centers the viewers attention.

.

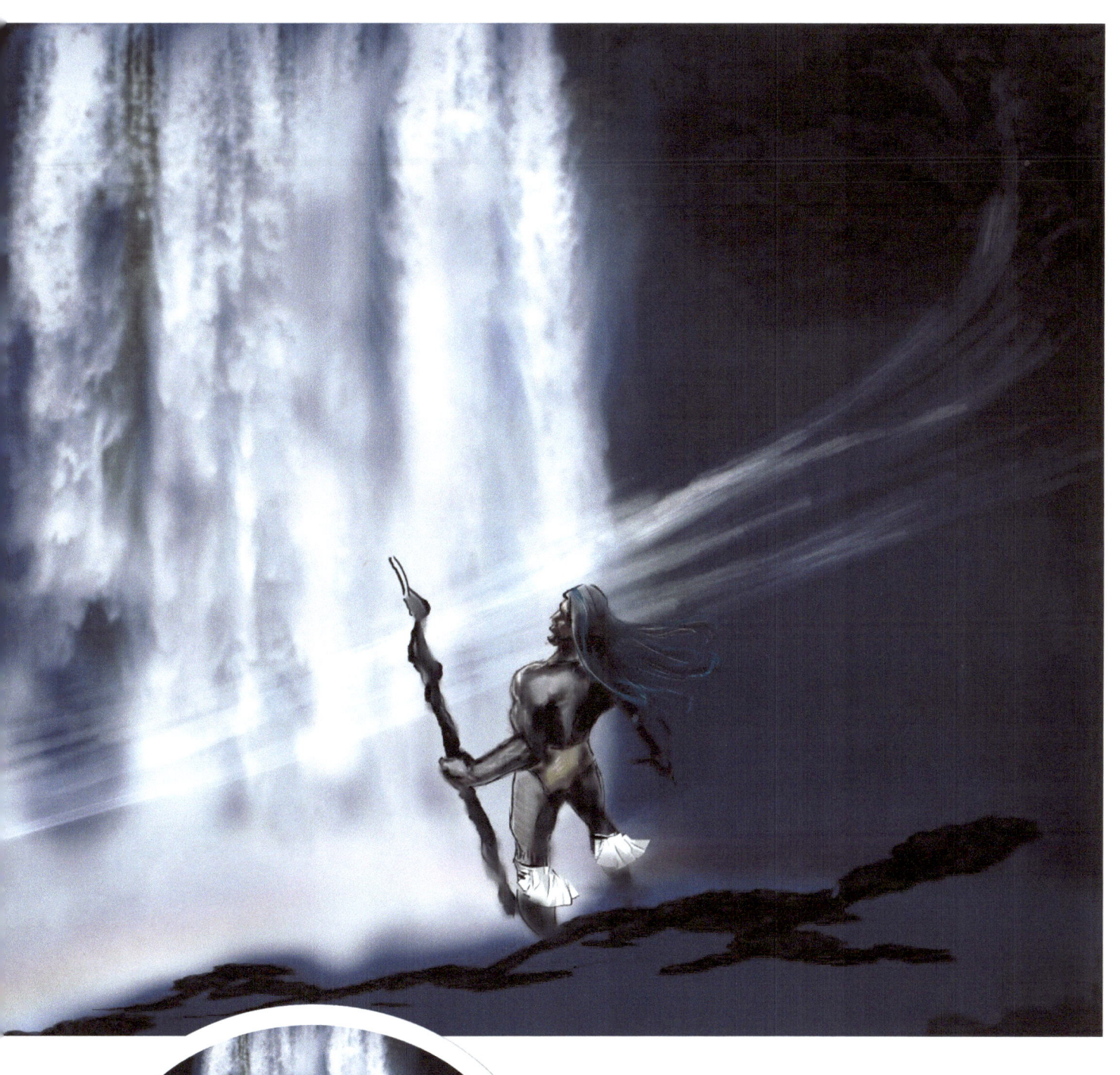

QUICK TIP

Blending and altering the saturation of the color of the water made it seem more transparent.

MAGIC TREE

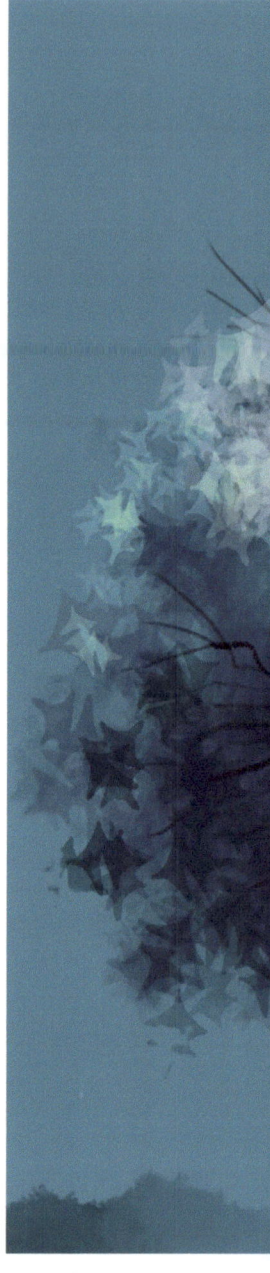

Making custom brushes for your artwork adds more of a sense of ownership to your design and adds additional tools to the toolbox.

The picture was inspired also by the significance of sacred places. In this case, the tree holds significant spiritual energy that the character down below is trying to channel with. The tree itself is a symbol of power and life in an otherwise barren land.

I used photo reference of a tree to capture all of the important details that I needed to include in the design. After I had the basic line art complete and I was happy with the composition, I added gradient map layers to add color to the entire design at once. I used a total of three and erased out areas where I wanted to add specific emphasis. The wisps are on a glow layer at the top of my layer stack. Some wisps are added under the glow layer and then blurred out so they appear farther away. The purple in the tree helps to create more depth and provide a little more variety.

I made my own custom leaf brush to paint in the leaves around the tree. Making custom brushes for your artwork adds more of a sense of ownership to your design and adds additional tools to the toolbox. Adding a character to the scene provides the viewer with a sense of scale for the design. It describes just how big the tree is compared to the people who dwell near it. Details like this would greatly assist a modeler to understand how to build this in 3D for use in a game environment or other entertainment purposes.

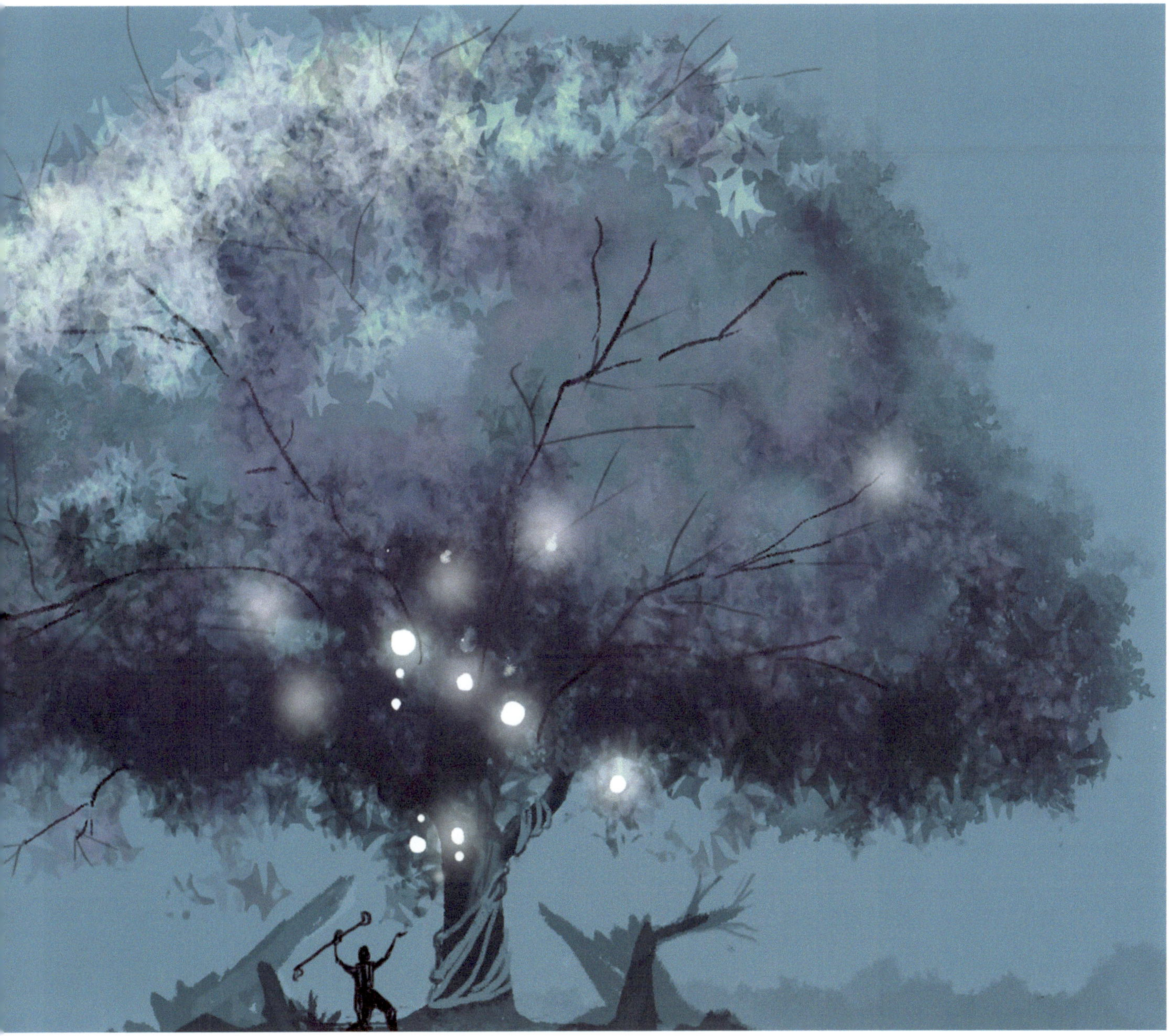

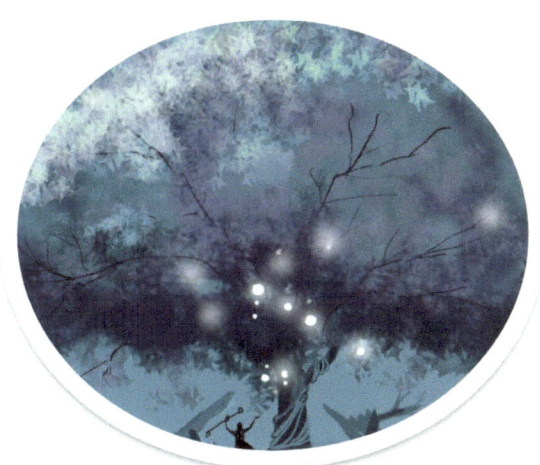

QUICK TIP

Glow layers an excellent way to make design elements really pop out. Dark background colors provide better contrast for the glow layer.

SCARECROW

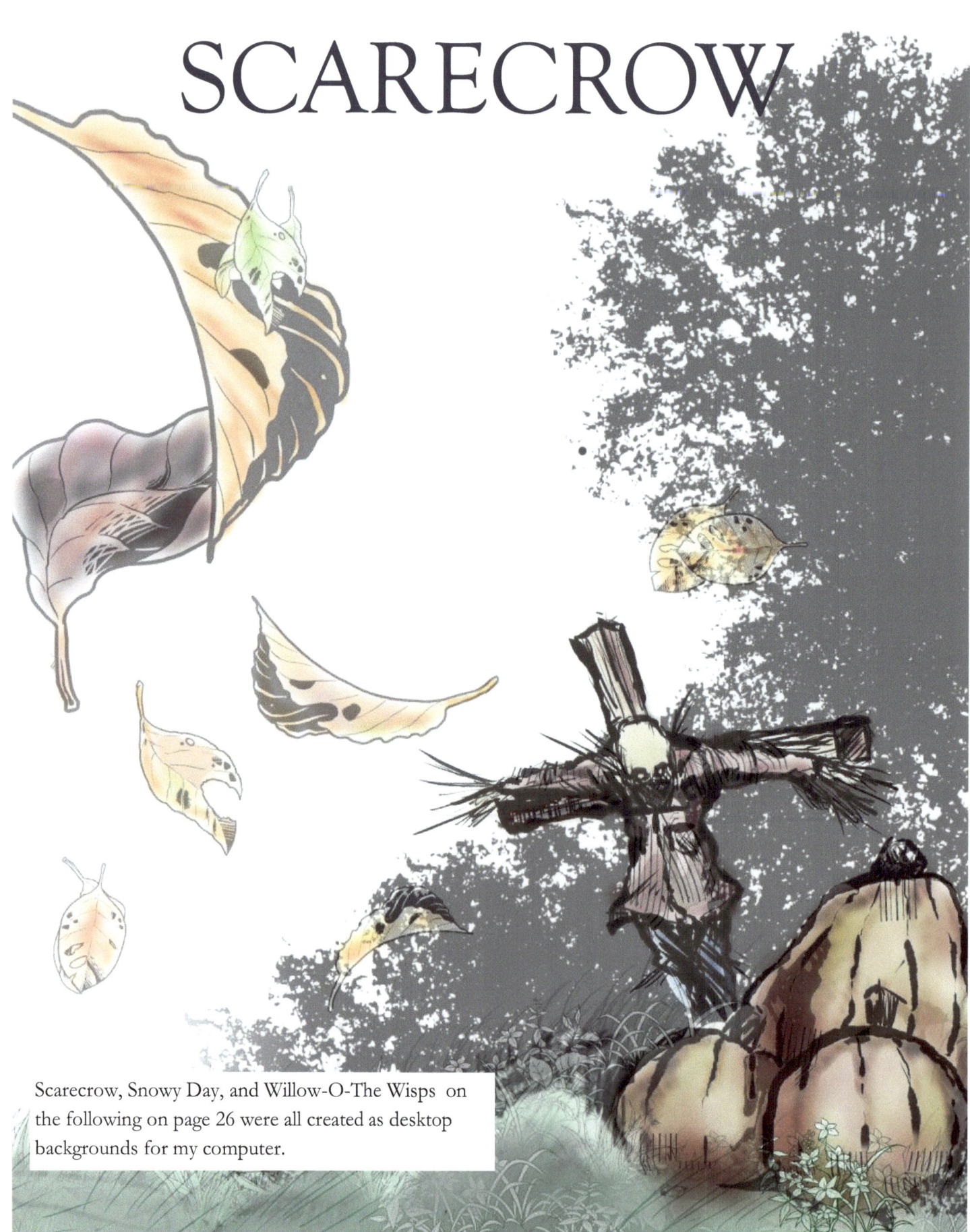

Scarecrow, Snowy Day, and Willow-O-The Wisps on the following on page 26 were all created as desktop backgrounds for my computer.

Snowy Day

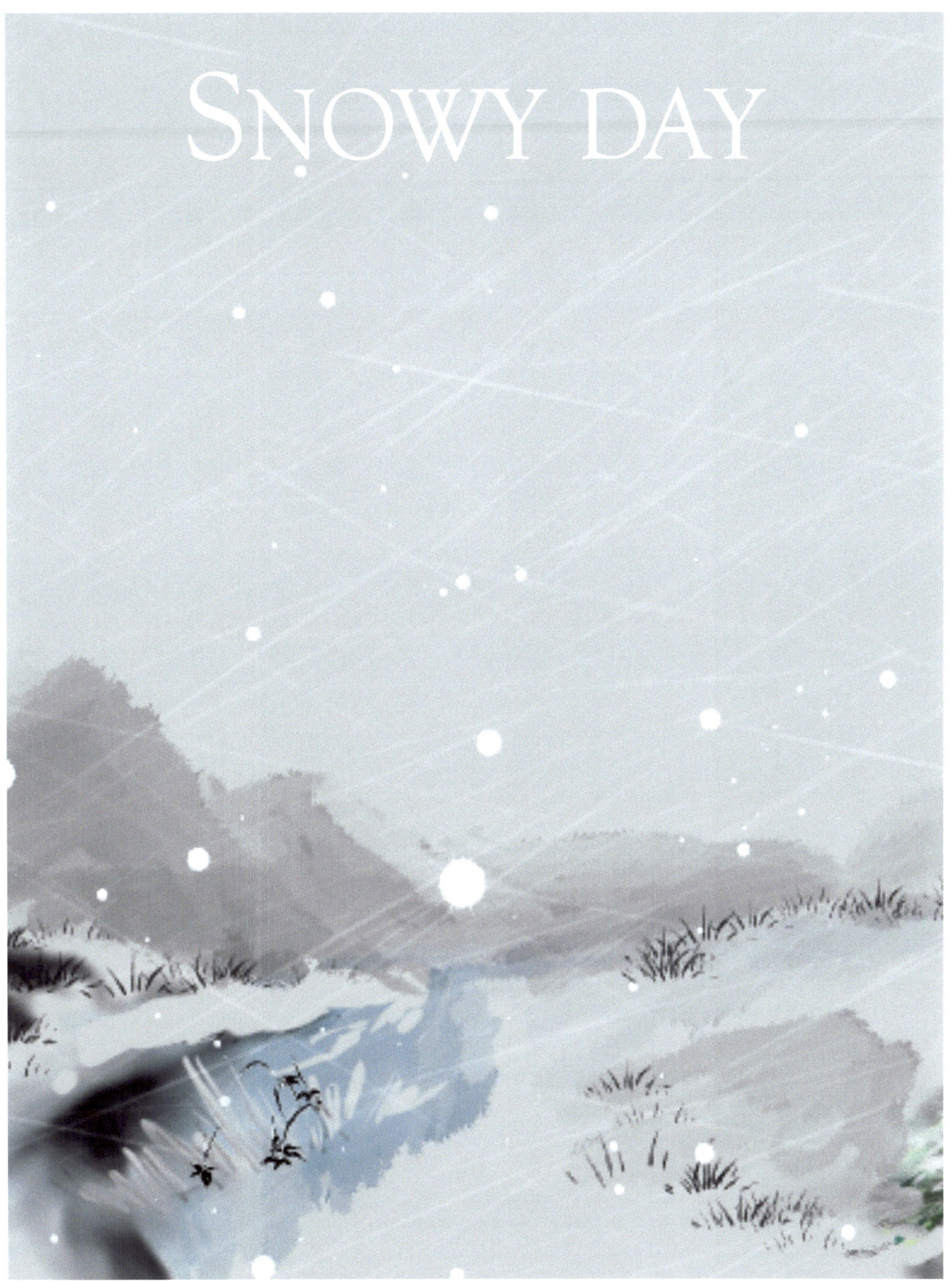

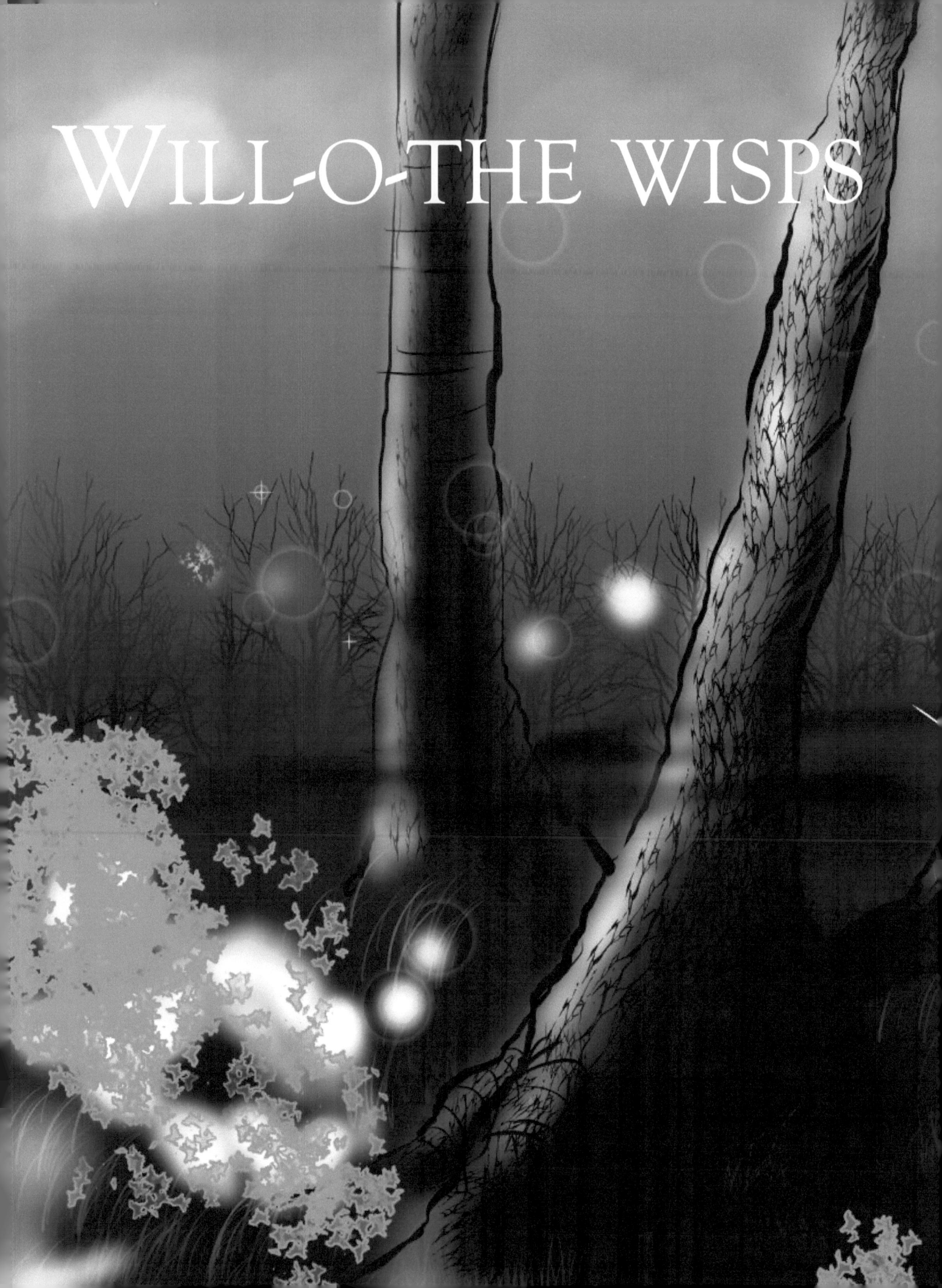

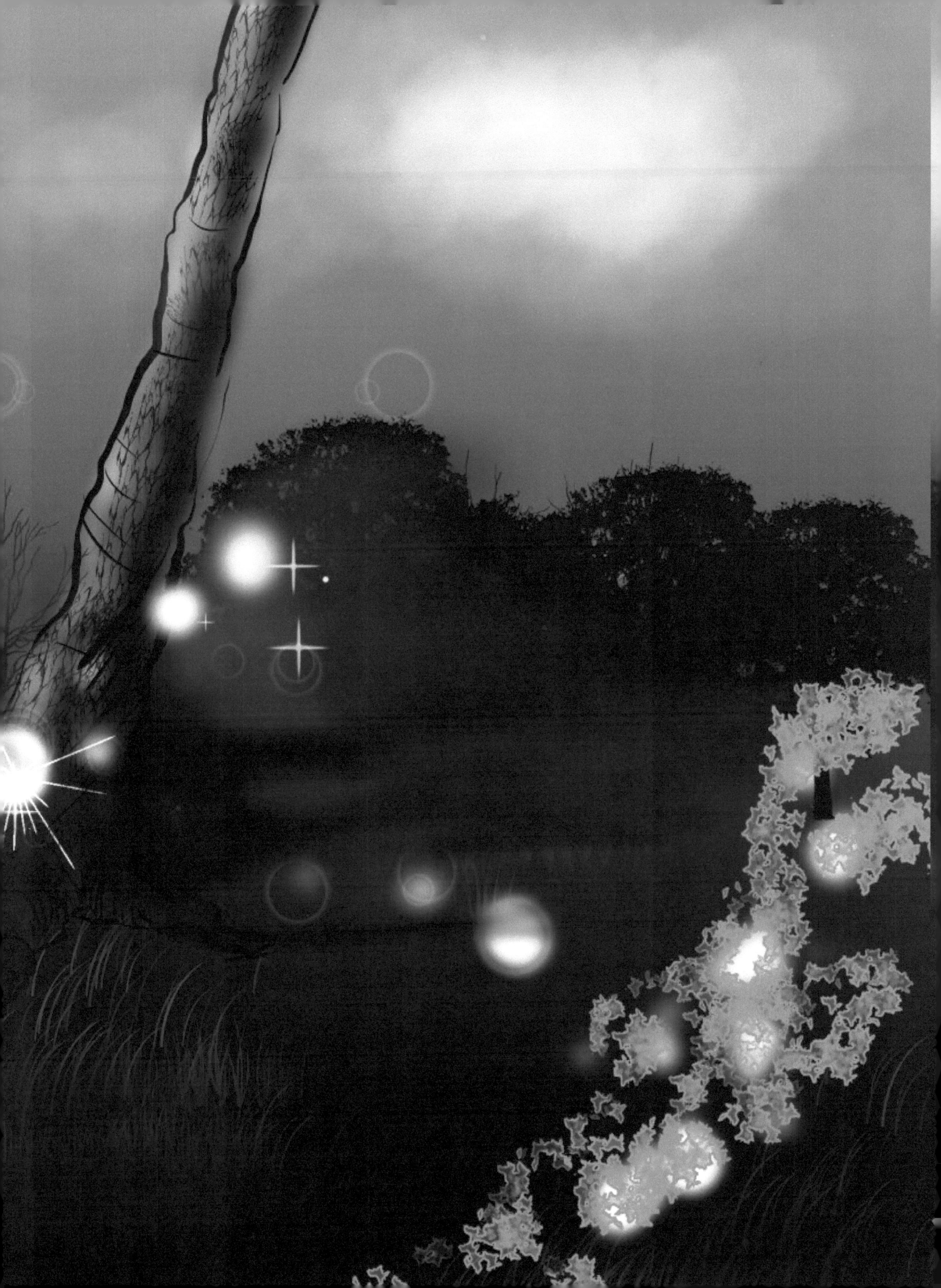

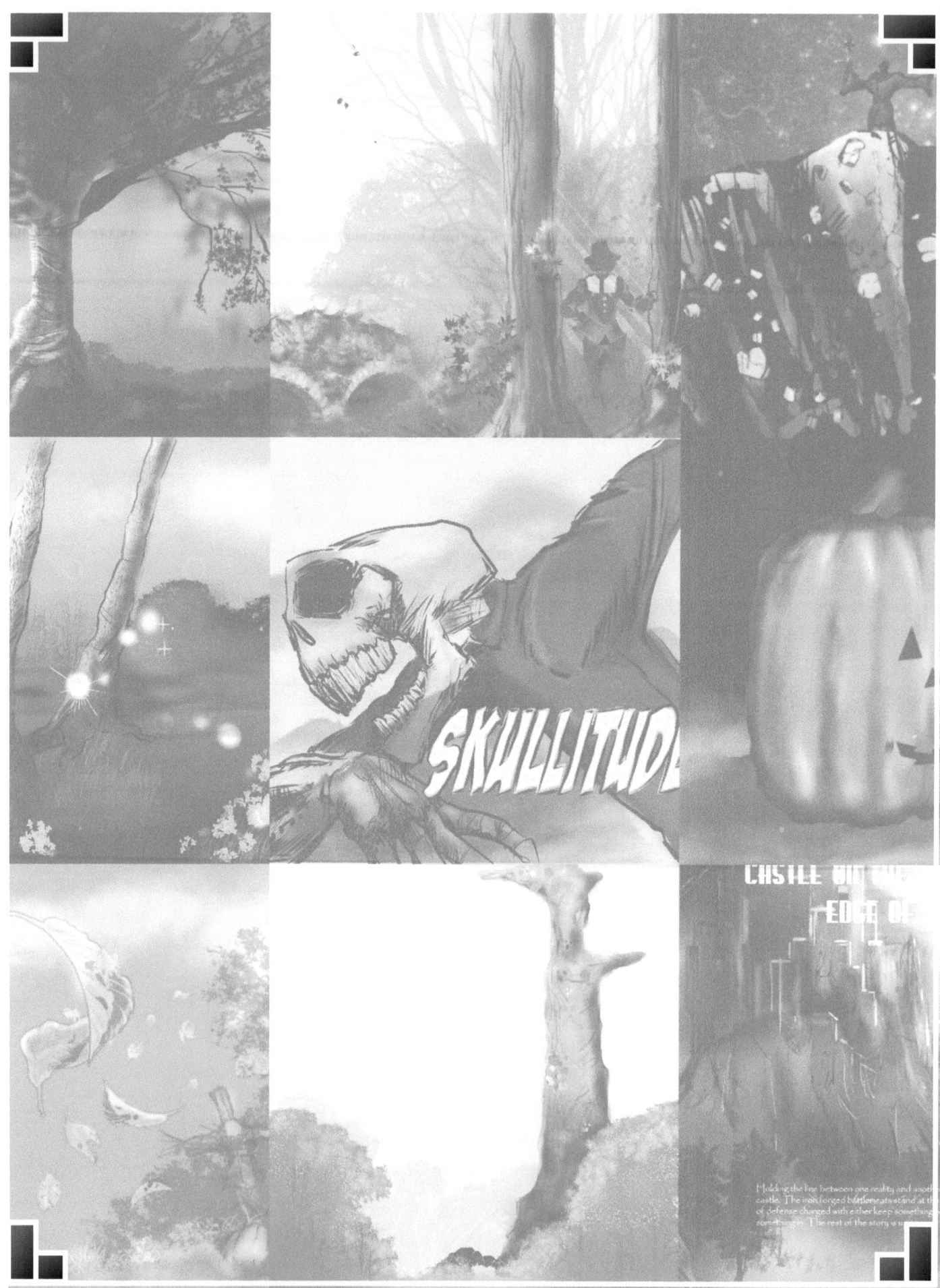

Logo Designs

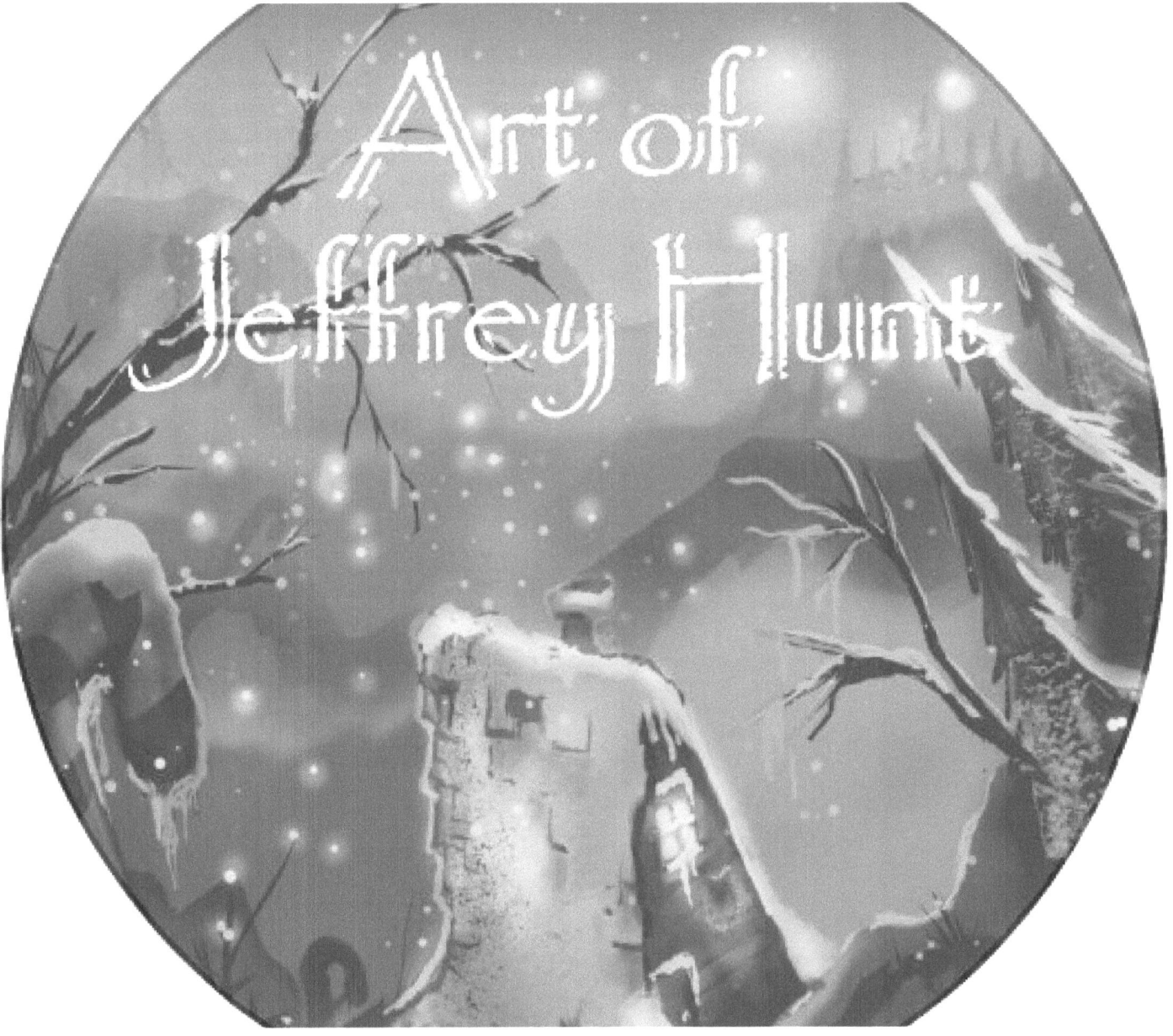

The next few pages are some samples of logos that I made from the paintings I already had. I make a logo template by creating a clipping mask at the top of my layer stack. Using a mask, only the painting will show through the area I defined. In this case, I filled a circle with color and the image only shows where a color has been applied.

These are additional logos I designed for separate projects including my own branding experiments. Masks are used with all of these to fit the design into the logo. The page on the right demonstrates a professional way to showcase your logos.

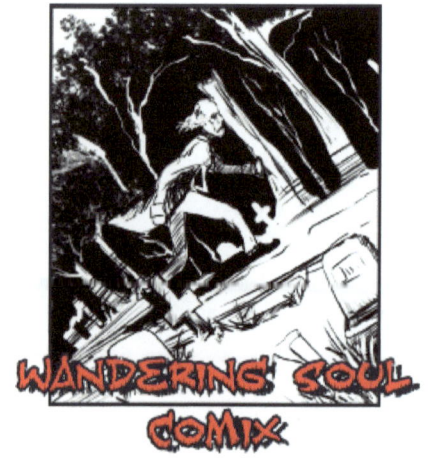

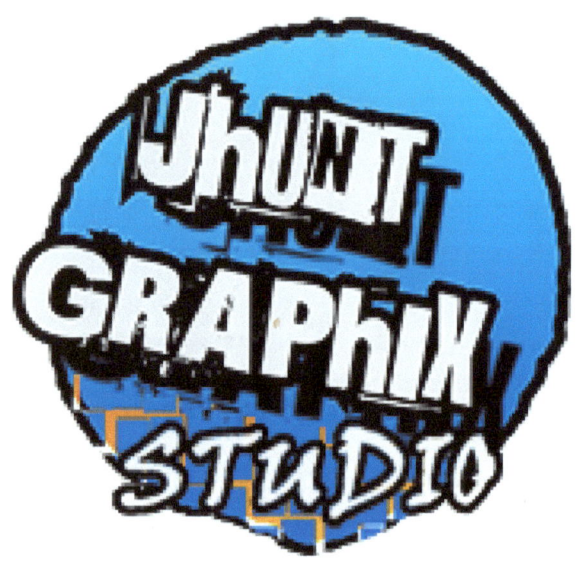

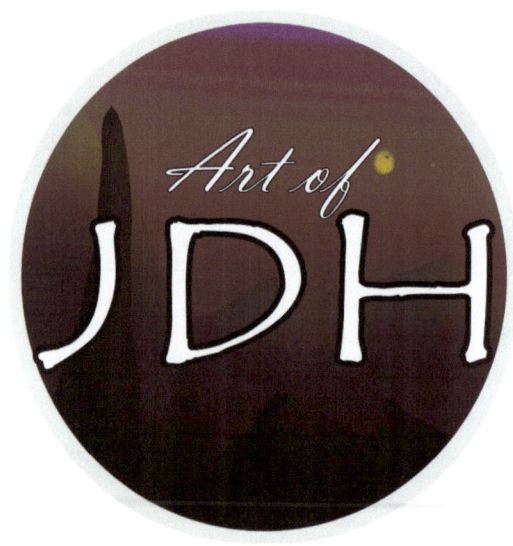

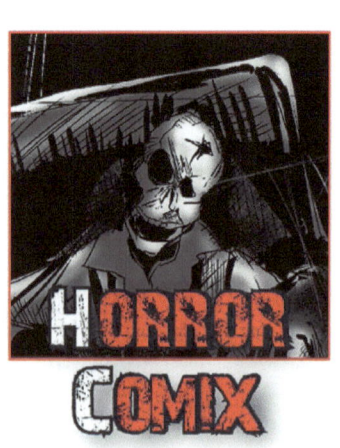

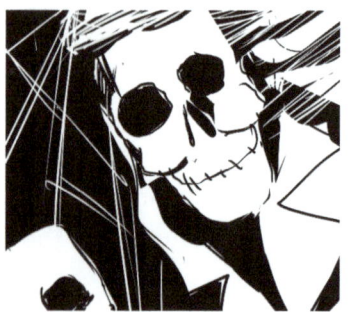

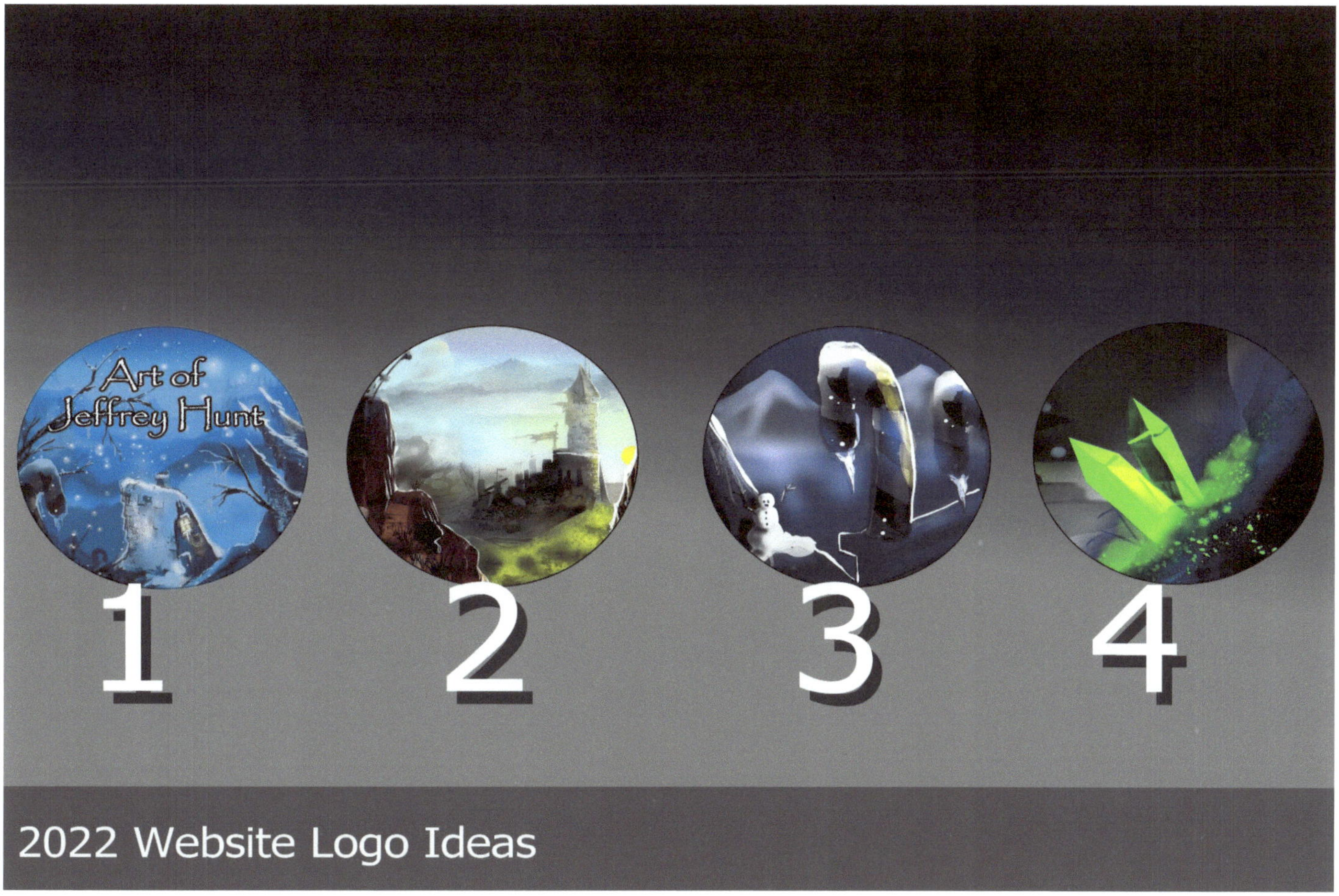

2022 Website Logo Ideas

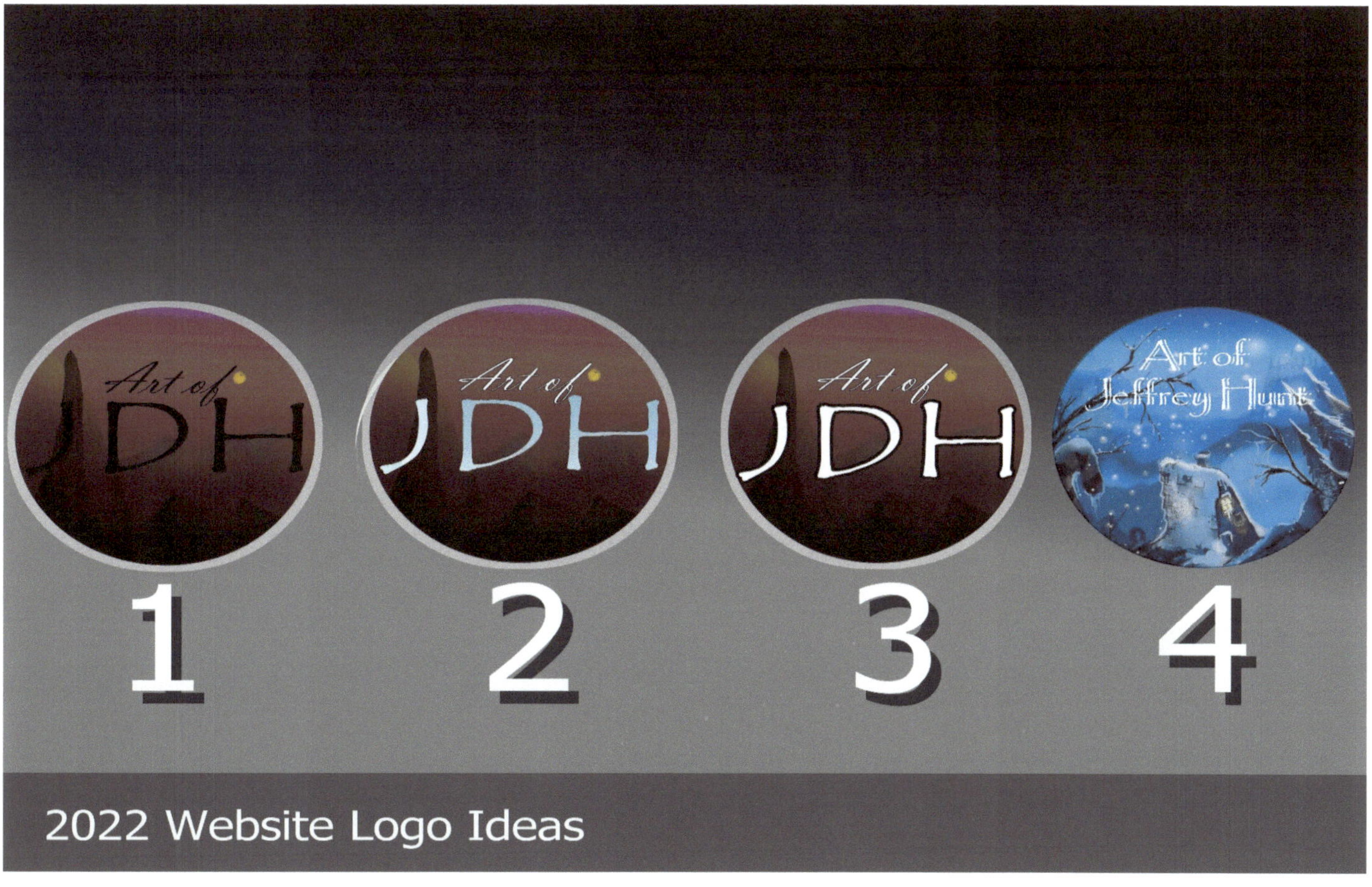

2022 Website Logo Ideas

Page 33

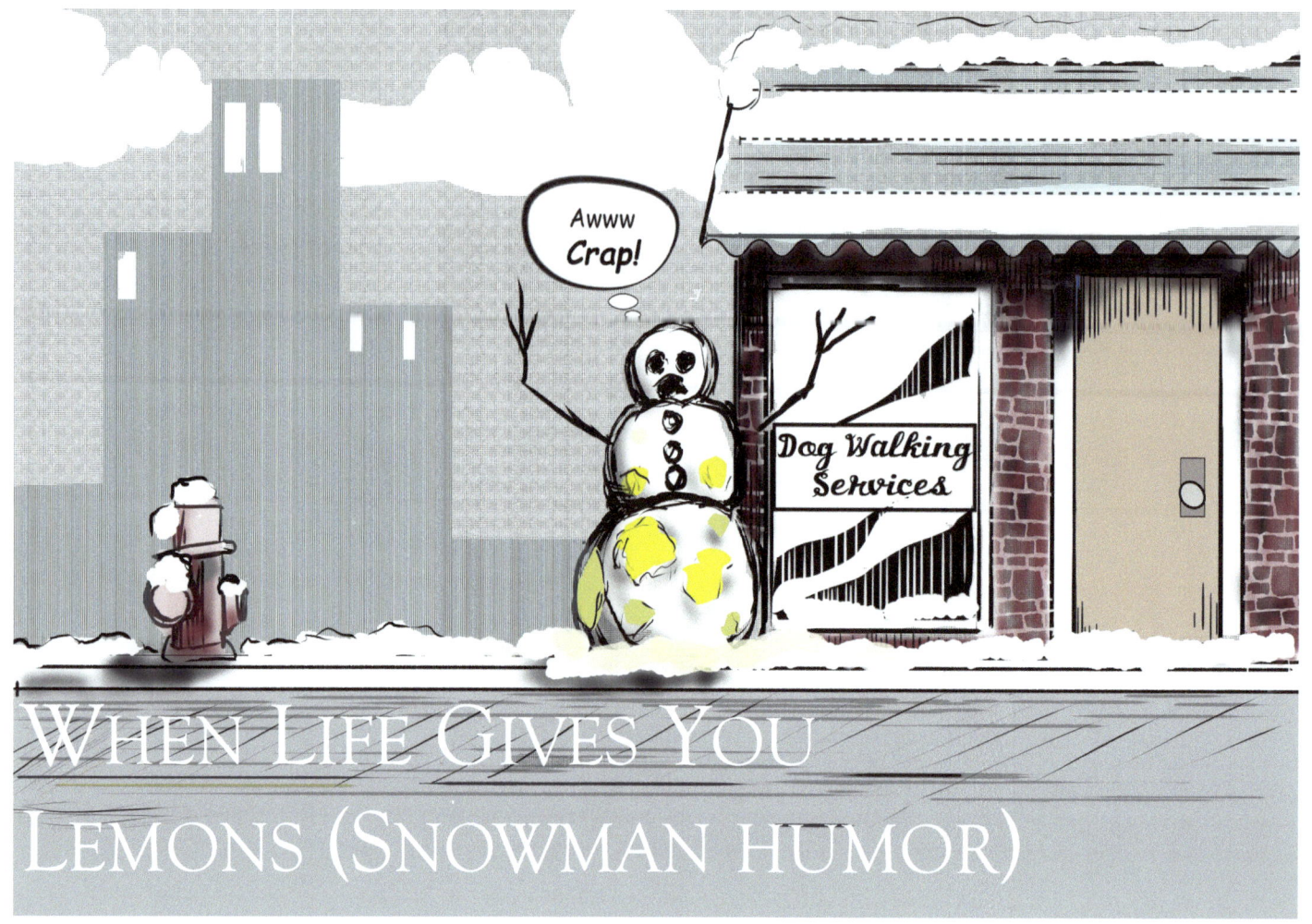

When Life Gives You Lemons (Snowman humor)

When life gives you lemons, you can certainly make lemonade or any other type of beverage you like. Challenges can come in all shapes and forms but how you handle them will enlighten you and provide you with growth so face them head on! As artists, there are lots of challenges to face such as time, subject matter, and inspiration to name a few.

Time

Time can be found through planning. I plan to give myself at least of a few hours to draw each day after coming home from a busy work day. It's not written anywhere or put into my phone calendar so that I don't feel stressed about it if I don't. Planning balanced with flexibility allows for better expectations. It's important for artists to determine their best mix of work-life balance. There is no proper formula but you don't want to leave your other commitments and family always on the backburner. I build a list of what I want to accomplish to help me stay on task when I am drawing so that I am as efficient as possible.

Subject Matter

Subject matter is not as much of a challenge as it used to be thanks to some of the YouTuber's out there who provide lots of ways of overcoming blank page syndrome. I still might spend a few minutes envisioning what I want to draw but after a few brush strokes, I'm off. But what do you do when you find yourself in a slump? Drawing exercises are a great way to get the creative energy moving in the right direction. Find images on the internet that you can use to draw. Drawing studies improve how you look at references and give you better understanding of study subject. Drawing trees from reference over and over again will help you draw better from memory. Save and collect your studies for reuse in other projects. A composite worksheet of all of your studies can save you time when building a new scene.

Inspiration

Inspiration to draw something that takes work. When you love to draw, it can come easier than those who don't draw often. The best inspiration comes to me from watching what happens around me and then just asking, "Hey, what if?" The snowman image I came up with was inspired by talking to my kids about all the funny things that could happen to a snowman. The rest was easy after that. I have to keep a notebook sometimes to keep track of the funny things they come up with.

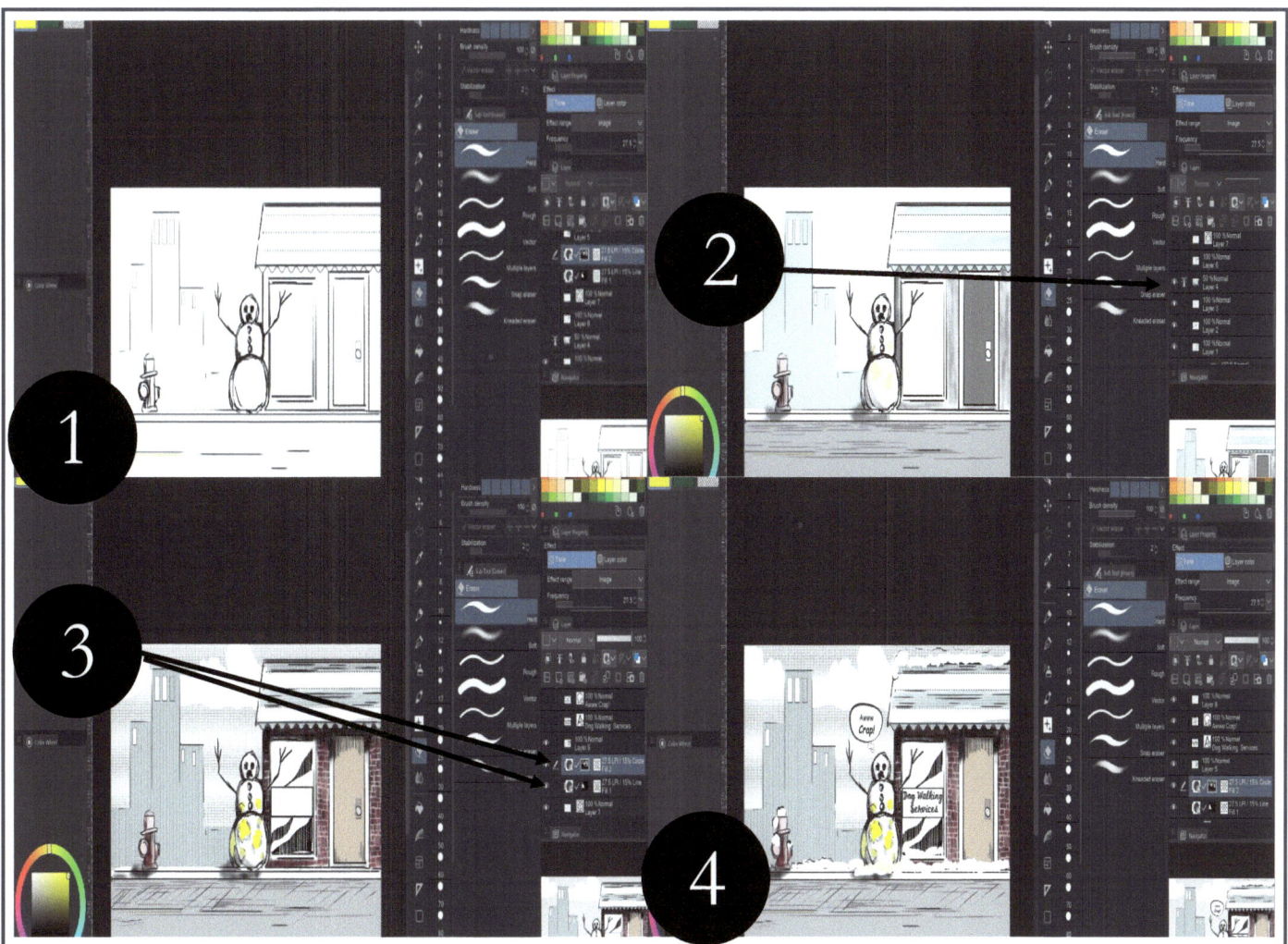

ABOUT THE DESIGN

1. I used a digital ruler to draw in the buildings and then freehanded the snowman using an inking brush. The inking brush produced a nice line quality. **2.** I set my inked layer as a reference (denoted by the symbol) so that I could use the bucket fill tool to add the color flats to the image. This is one of the most efficient ways to add color to a drawing. I also reduced the opacity to 50% so that I could concentrate on just the color. **3.** I added texture to the buildings using separate layers for the sky, the buildings in the back and the brick pattern in the foreground building. This helps define the texture by adding details so that the elements in the drawing help the viewer understanding what they are looking at. **4.** Final details such as the snow and the lettering were added to the building along with the thought balloon.

Page 35

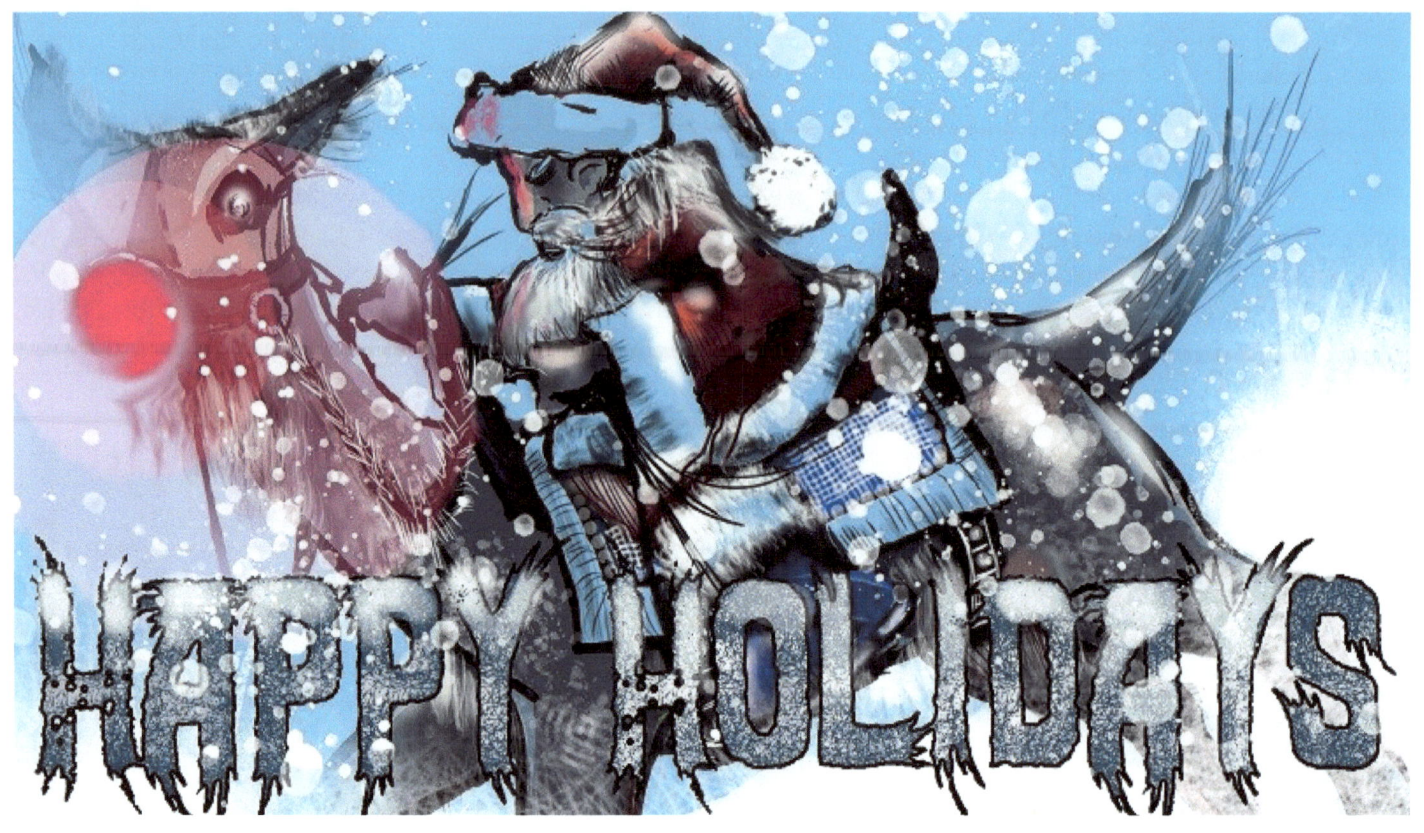

This Christmas design was used to turn a regular blog post into a Christmas card that I could post on social media. The design was made using Photoshop and it was one of the first times I ever used it. I find that it is important as an artist to be as versatile with as many different types of tools that are available out there. It bears repeating. On the following page is the inked line art prior to adding in the colors. If you look very close, you will notice small breaks in the line art. It's very important that if you are using a fill tool of any sort that you close all those breaks in your lines. If you don't the software can get "confused" and the entire image will have the selected color applied.

How do you solve this? There are features such as "close and fill" that can still allow you to fill an area with a break depending on how the settings are selected. A bit of trial and error will have to be used to get it just right. The bottom image on the right shows the completed colors and shading. When I color, I always make sure that the color layer is under the inked layer so that the lines are still visible.

The bright nose of the reindeer is a glow layer and a screen layer. The glow layer is the nose itself where the glow would be the brightest. The screen layer is below it providing an additional ambient glow around it. This layer allowed the red light to coat the surroundings much like a colored light bulb would color a room.

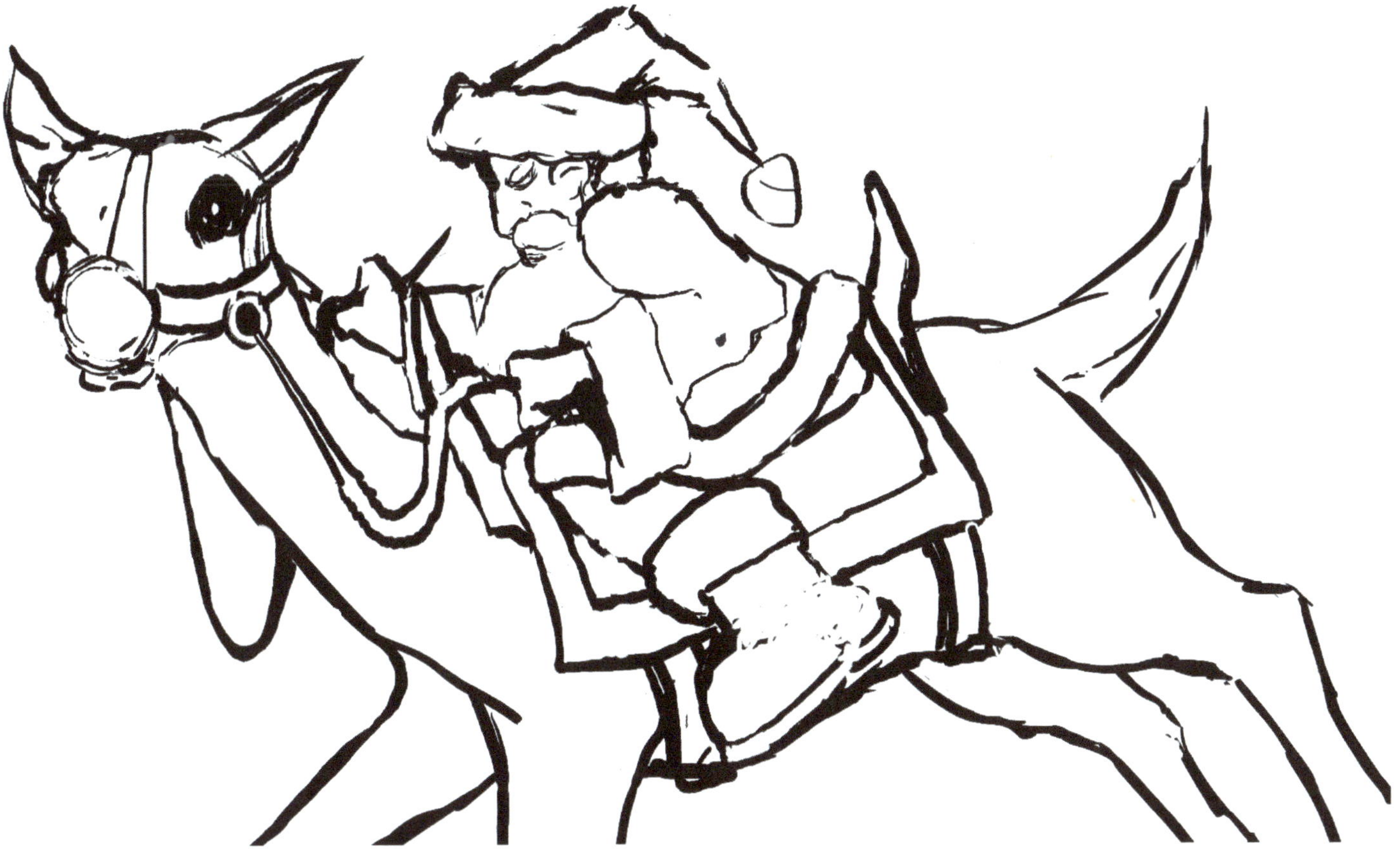

Above: Inked line art with small breaks in the line to demonstrate coloring challenges.

Below: Completed coloring and shading of the image using overlay and screen layers.

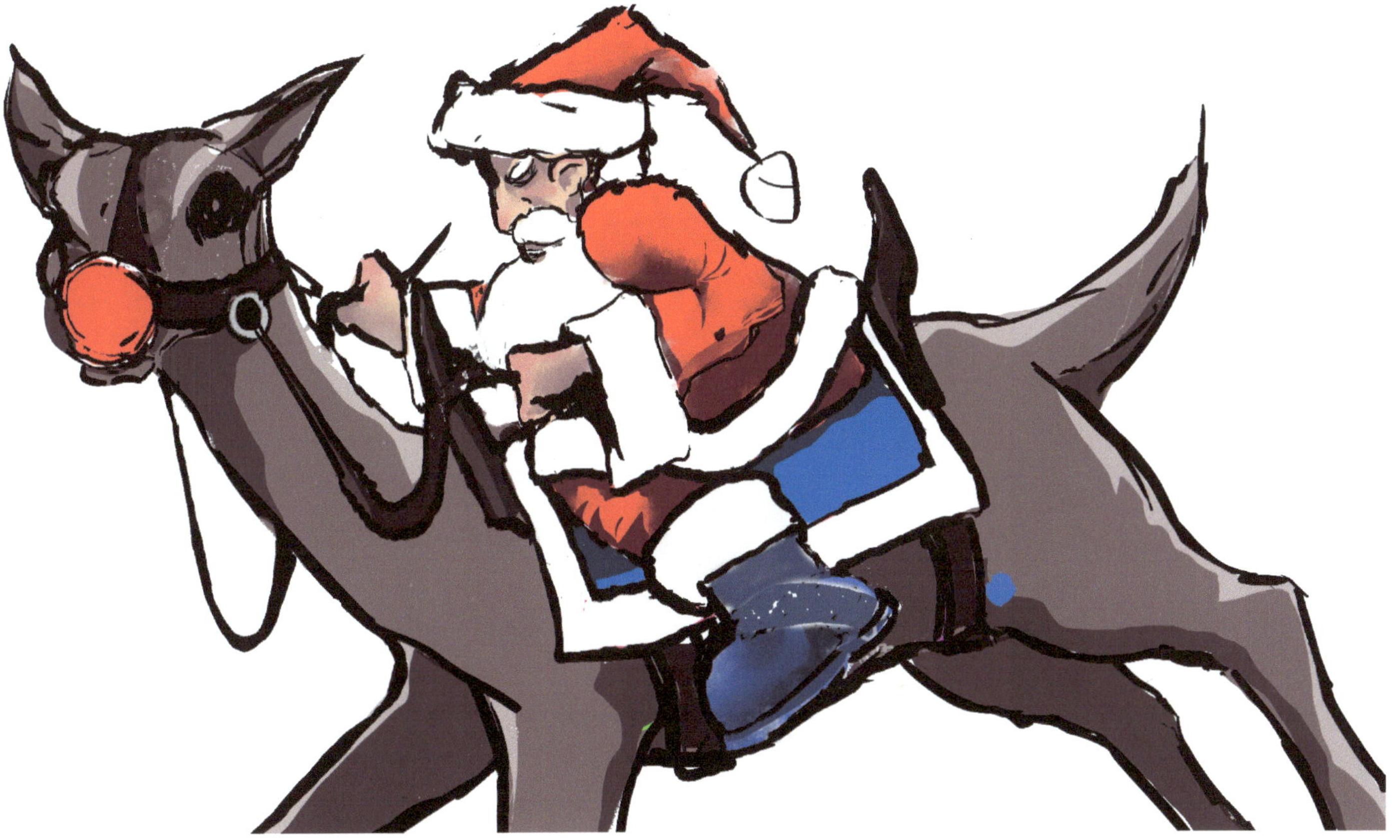

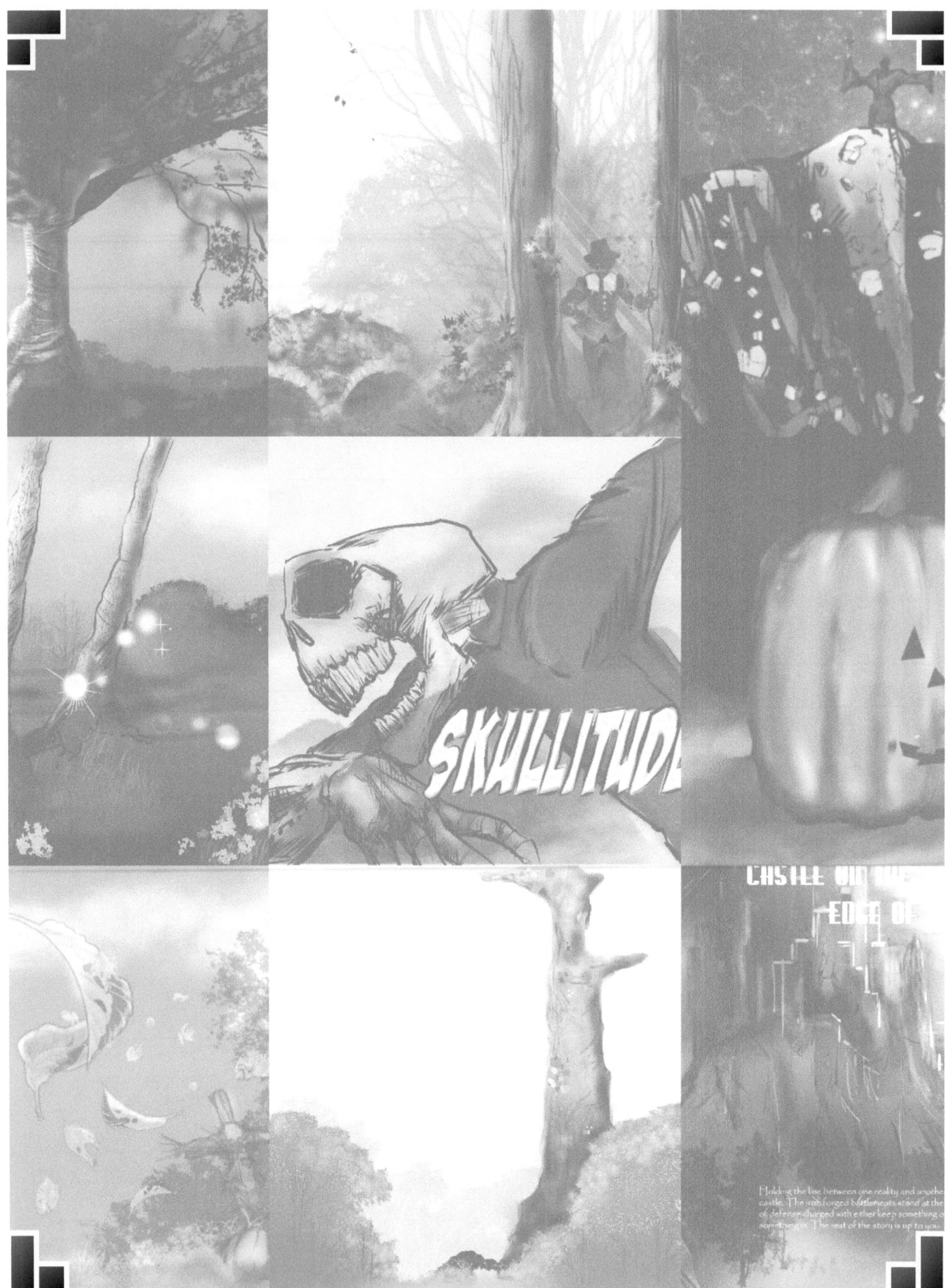

Character Concepts and Animations

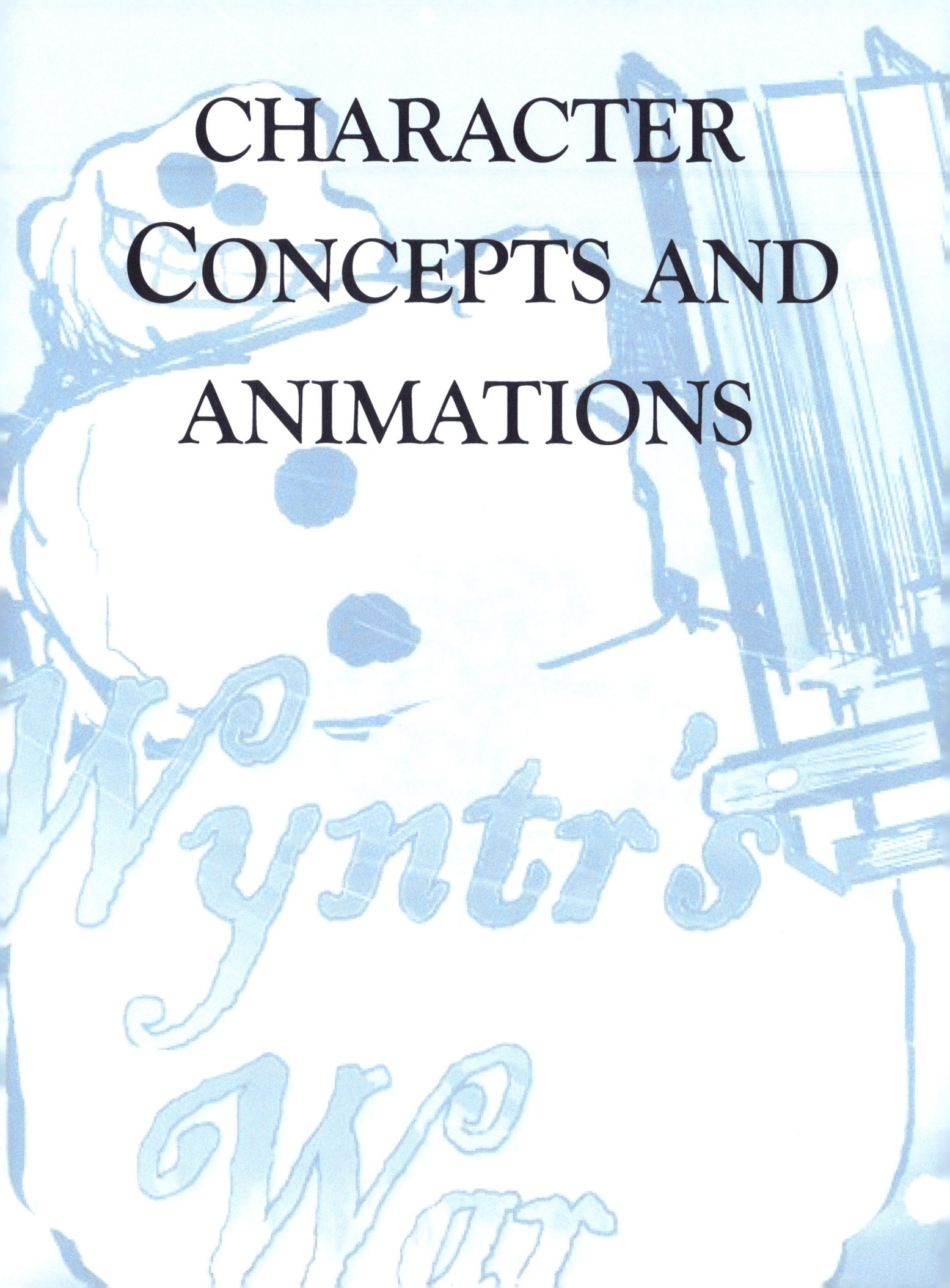

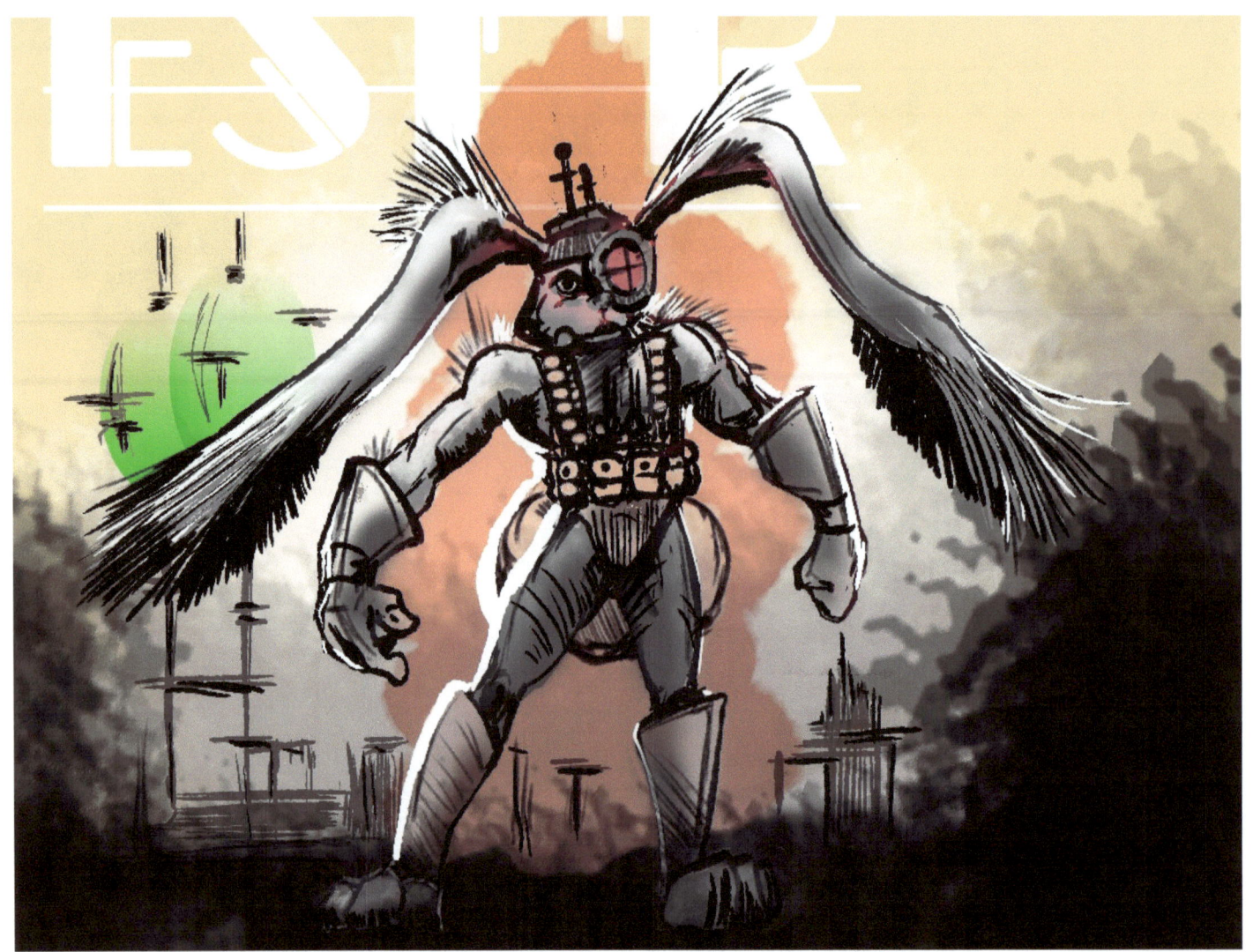

More character design concepts in the works for future stories. EST'R is the story about a cybernetically altered rabbit trying to survive on a the war-torn planet. The hero in this story is a reluctant one who finds himself in lots of difficult situations as he strives to find himself and becomes critical to the very future of the planet.

The design goals in the image on top and on the right were to create a painterly watercolor effect under the inks. In the first image up top the bright orange-pink color helps center the viewers eye on the main character. The watercolor smoke in the distance adds depth to the background and was painted in on a separate layer with a lower opacity.

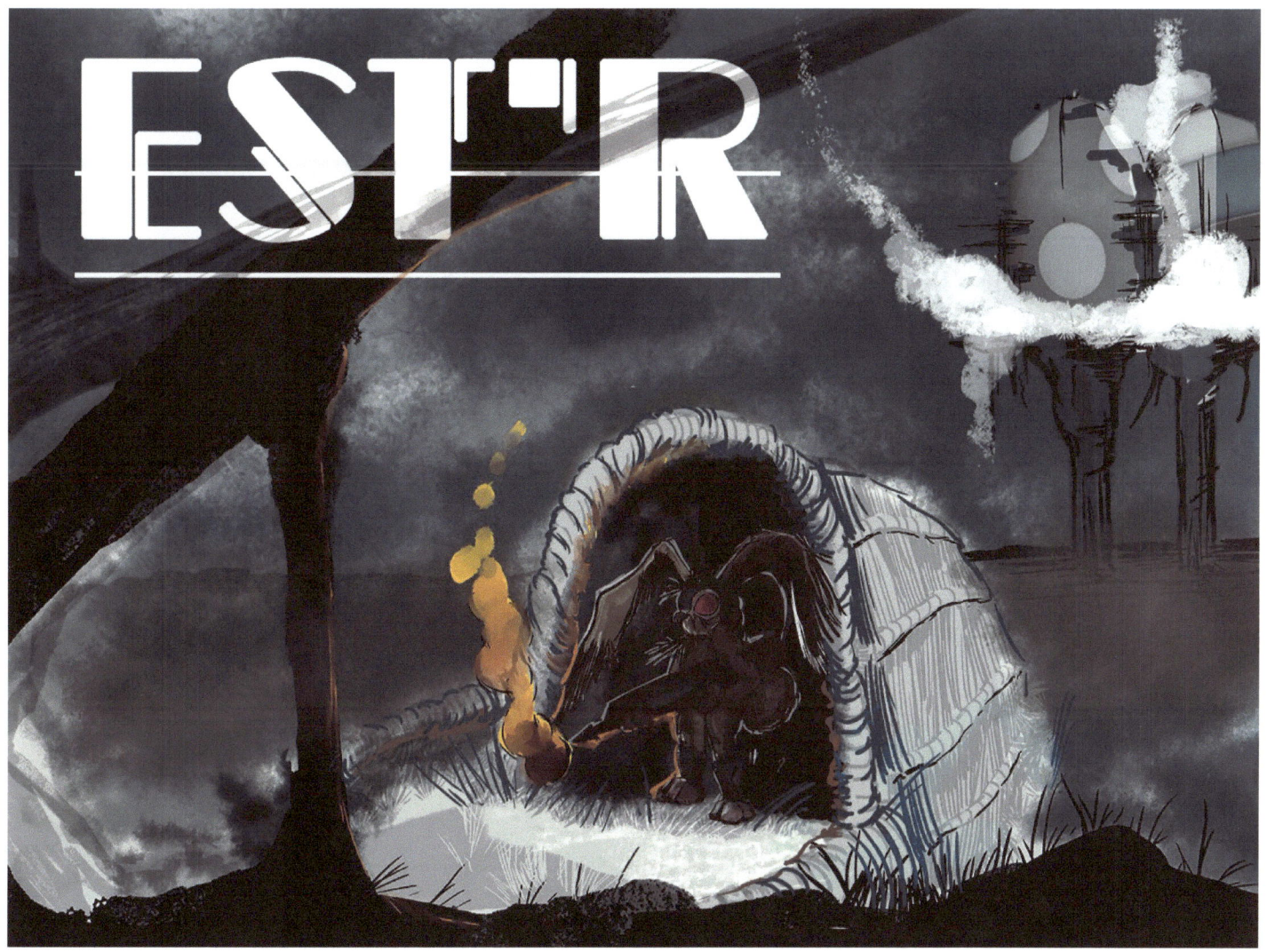

The image on top is a darker nighttime design. The rock formation in the front is the darkest and makes it pop out more against the duller colored background. An orange color again is used to provide a focal point and provide some cool light reflections off the character and the rock in the front. Again, I'm trying to get a more watercolor affect like you would on real paper with the actual paint.

Why not just use real watercolor on regular paper? C'mon man. Digital art is the wave of the future and its all about being able to use the tools to work efficiently. I have a ton of respect for those who still practice actual paint to paper to make illustrations though. I think that those are truly beautiful too. The next two pages are miscellaneous character designs.

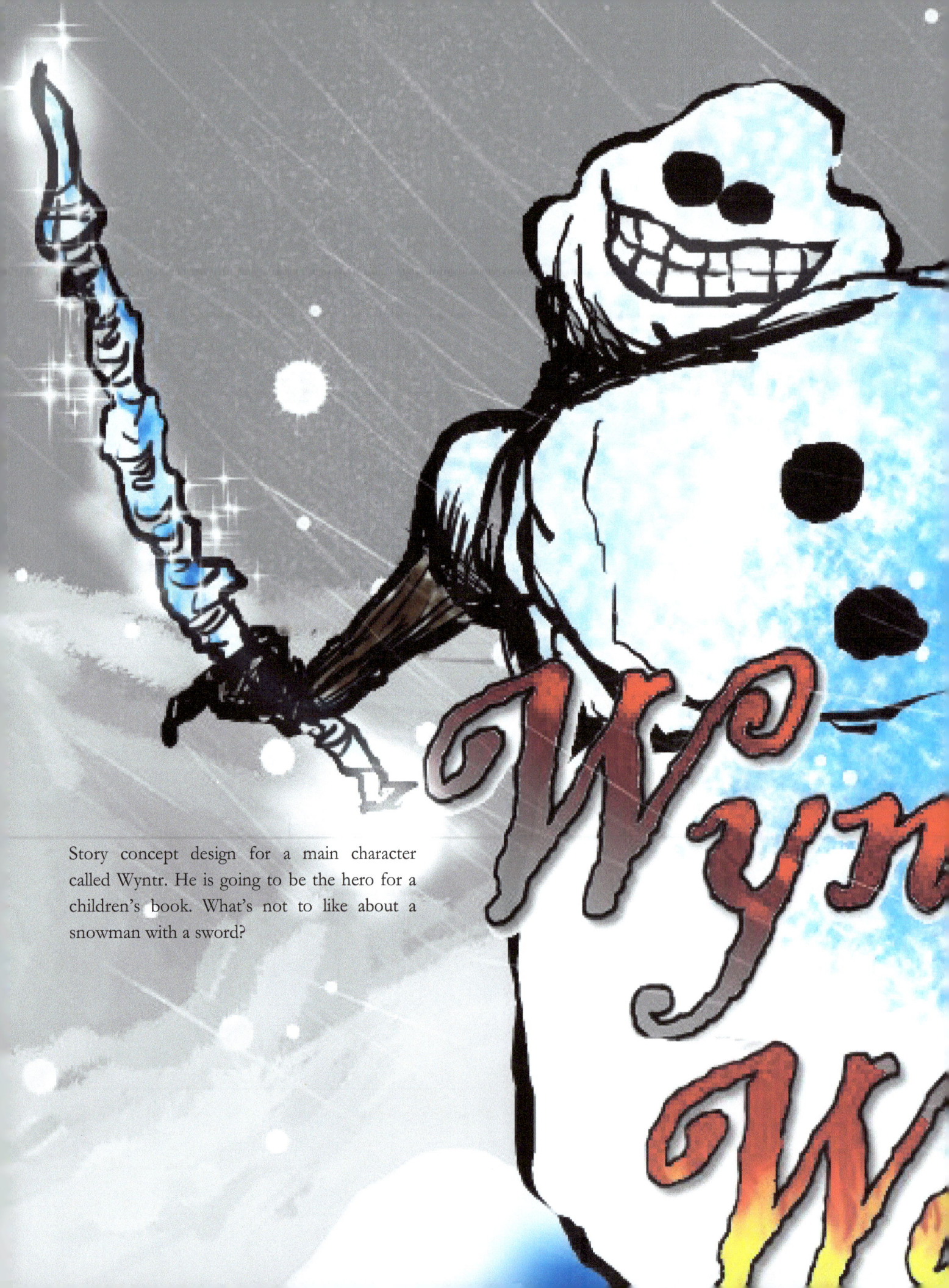

Story concept design for a main character called Wyntr. He is going to be the hero for a children's book. What's not to like about a snowman with a sword?

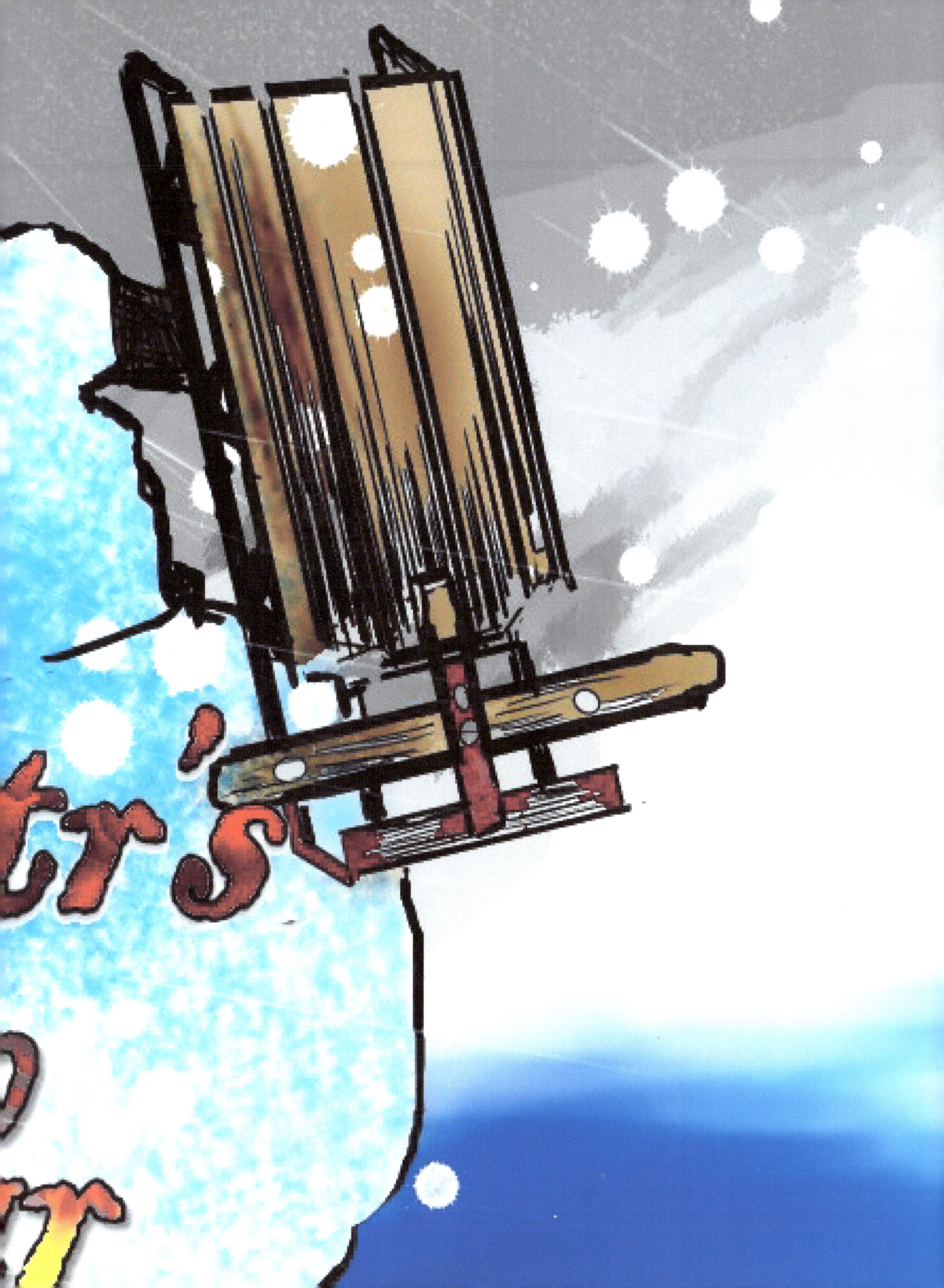

Ghost in the Machine

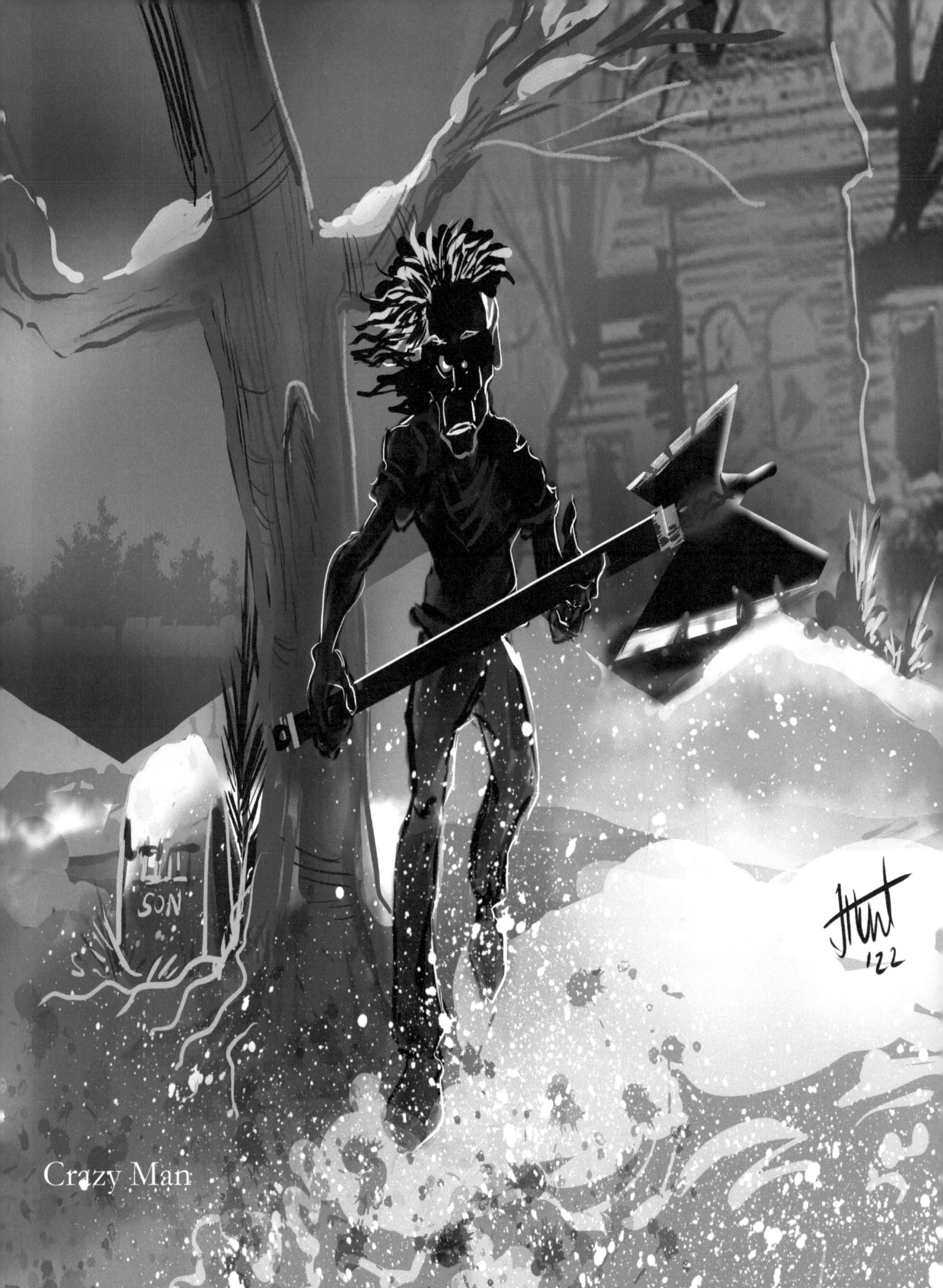

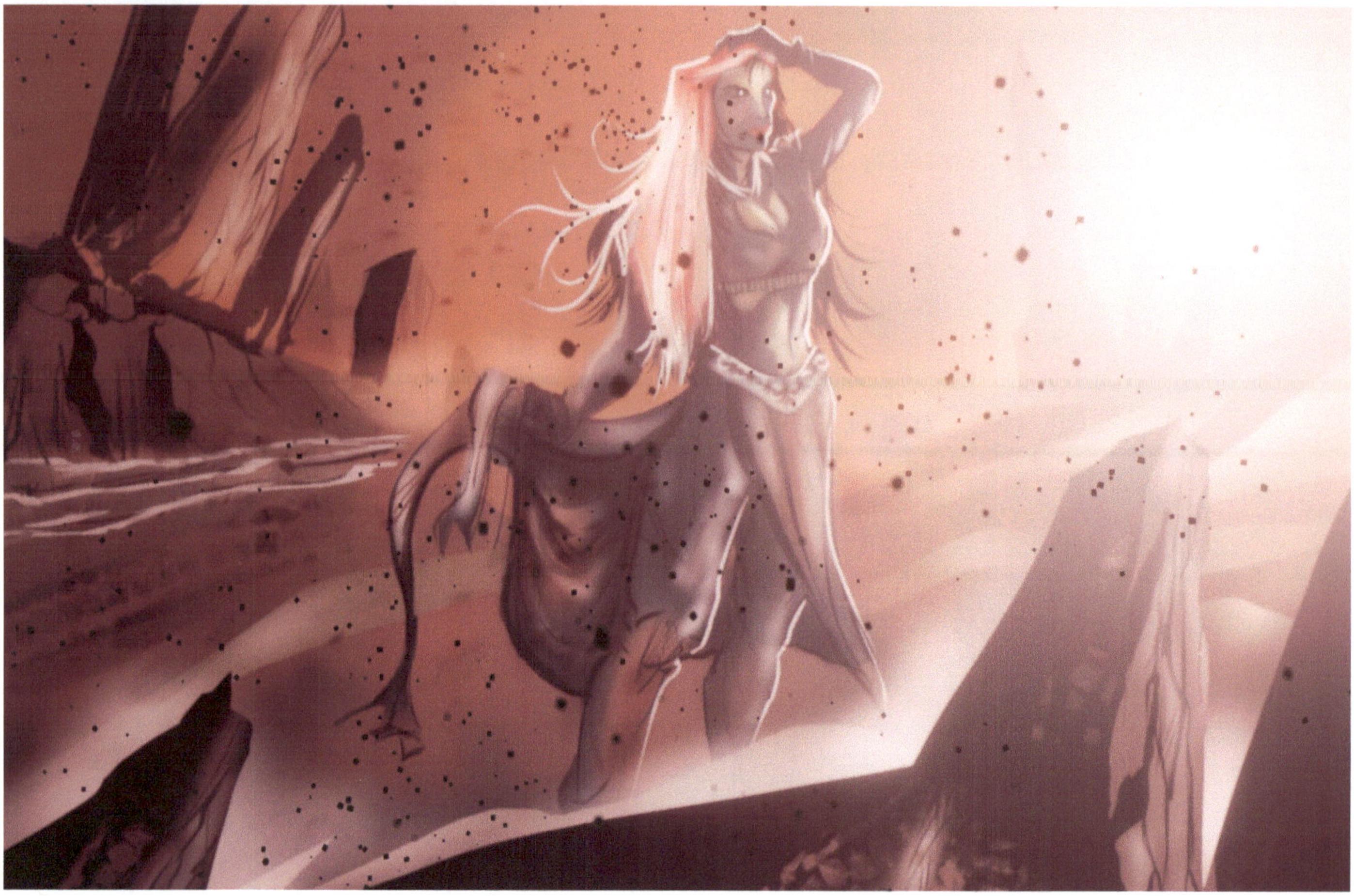

Using Clip Studio Paint and Blender to Animate

As an artist, it's very important to utilize all of the tools out there…and boy are there a lot. Blender and Clip Studio Paint work very well together in that you can start a project in one application and finish it up in another. Most folks I know create grey boxes in Blender, export them, and then import them into their favorite drawing program where they create their final illustration.

The design is about 25 layers using many correction layers as I went to adjust color and aesthetic for the overall design. This was created using Clip Studio Paint for the digital drawing / painting process.

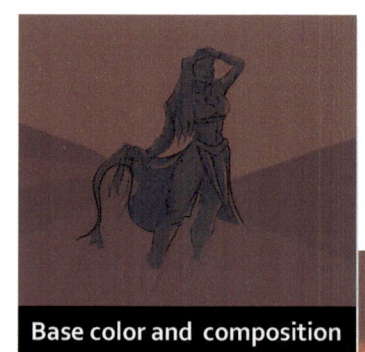
Base color and composition

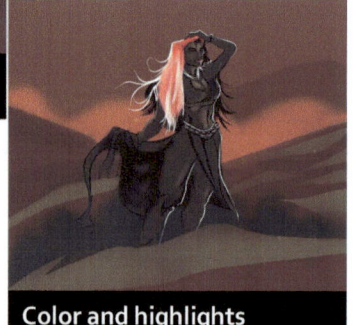
Color and highlights

During the final polishing stage I really go to town to define as many details as possible. Knowing where the focal point is key because you don't want to add too many details to areas in the design that are farther away. It's best to keep the fine details toward where you want the viewer to look. Materials are also better defined to properly reflect light the way they would realistically. For example, a knight's armor is much more reflective than the clothing of our desert witch here. As such, only ambient bounce light is considered.

The background is mainly rock but as you can see, they get lighter and less detailed the farther back that they go. The shapes of the darker rocks in the foreground were used to help center the composition of the character in the scene.

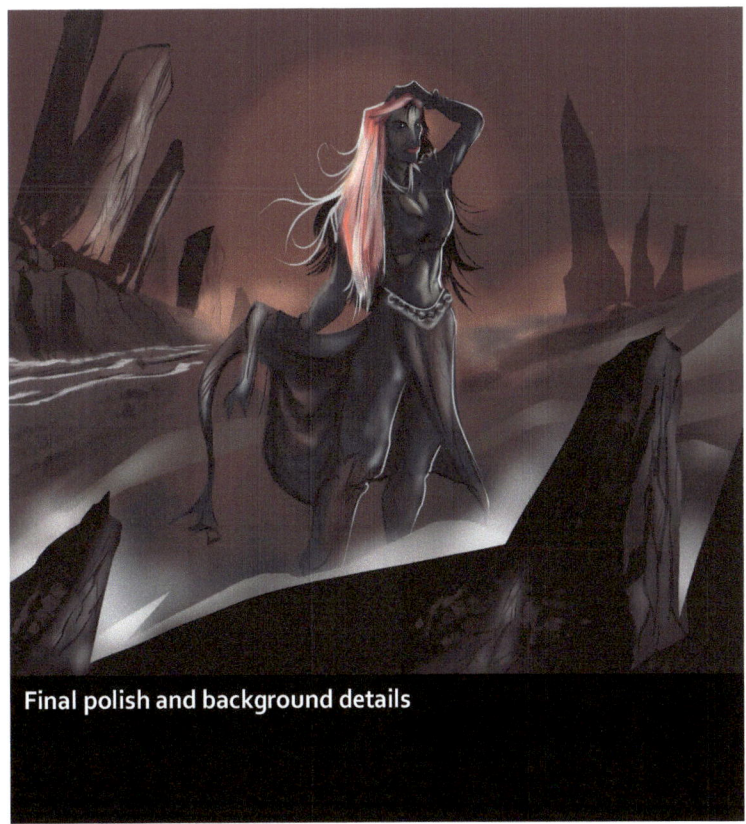
Final polish and background details

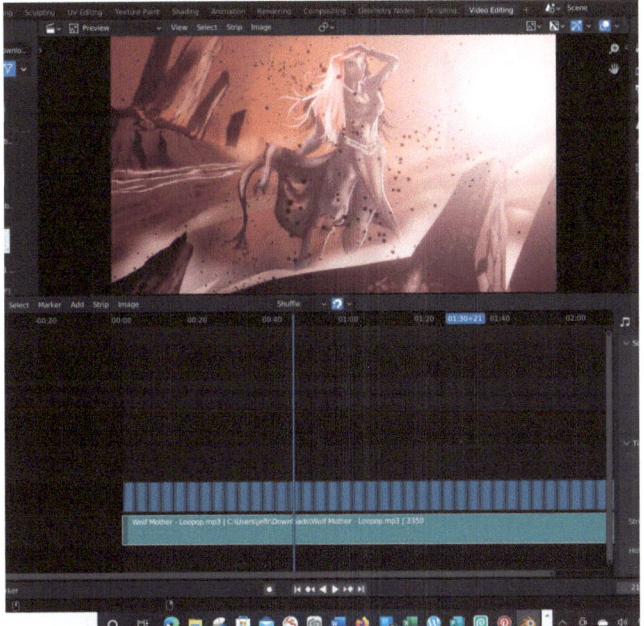
Blender's compositor was used to add the music to the animation in the final stage and then combined into a MP4

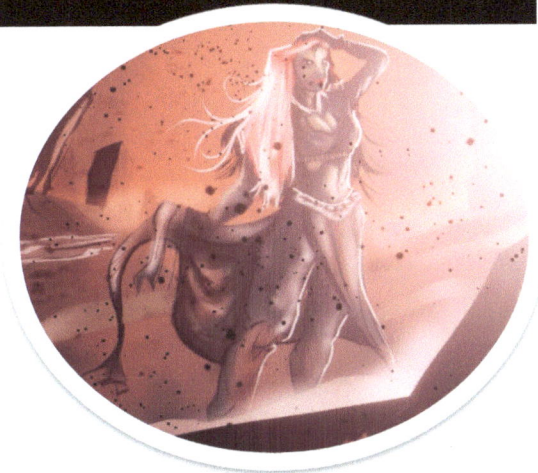

I uploaded the finished .png into Blender and added some additional lighting effects. For this design, I then created a particle field to simulate the effects of being in a desert sand storm of some sort. The light which I set to 1500W, really sets off the glow that I was looking for and color matched very nicely with her clothes and other highlights. I just love the versatility I get when I use Blender. Experiment with different lighting setups. The lights have the effect of adding a gradient map layer to your designs in Clip Studio Paint. You could almost completely change your color scheme around from the design that you started from.

The next two pages are of similar projects.

QUICK TIP

Creating templates in Blender for your 3D setups will save you time as you go. You can just change out the picture in the same simulation

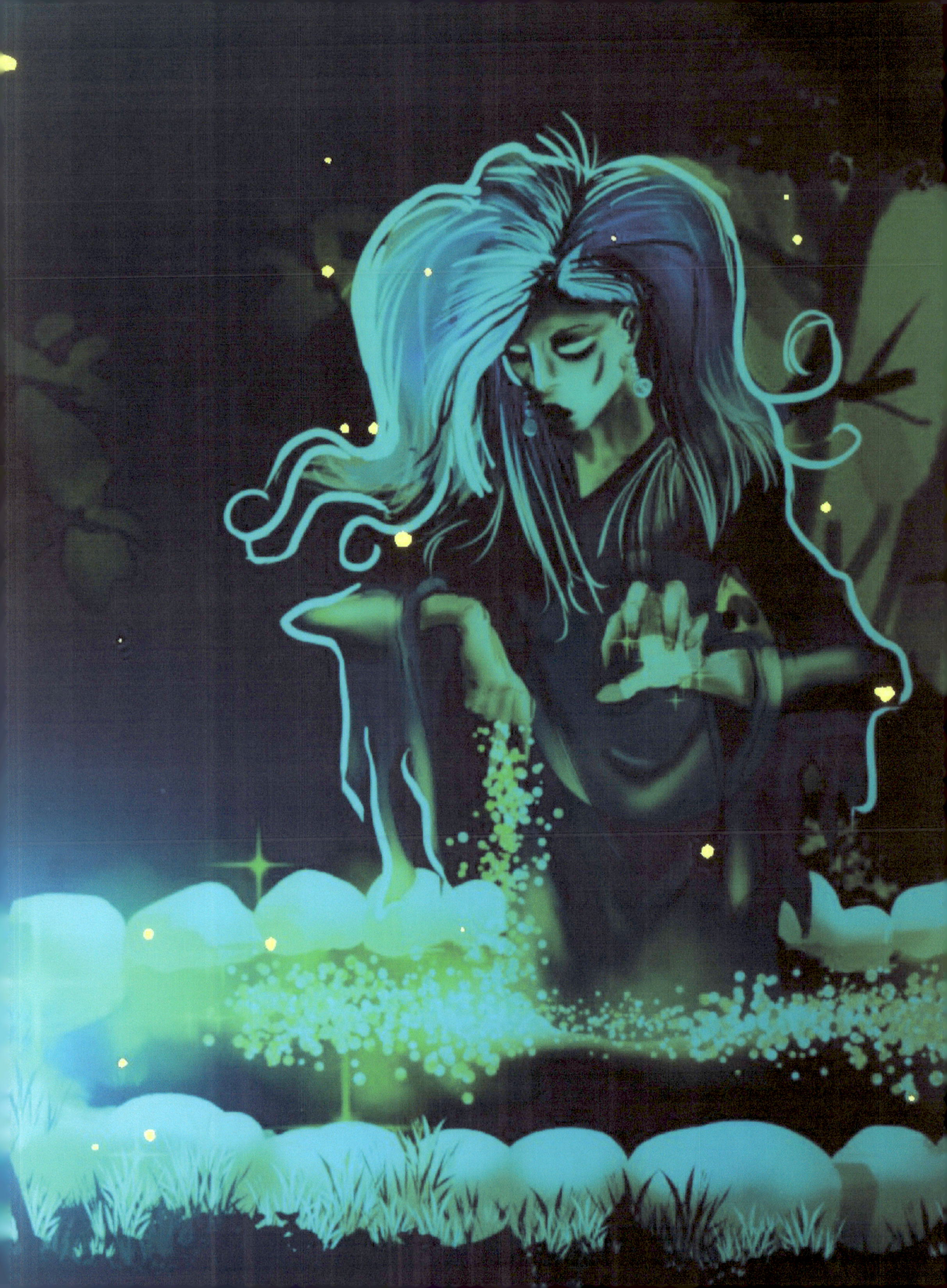

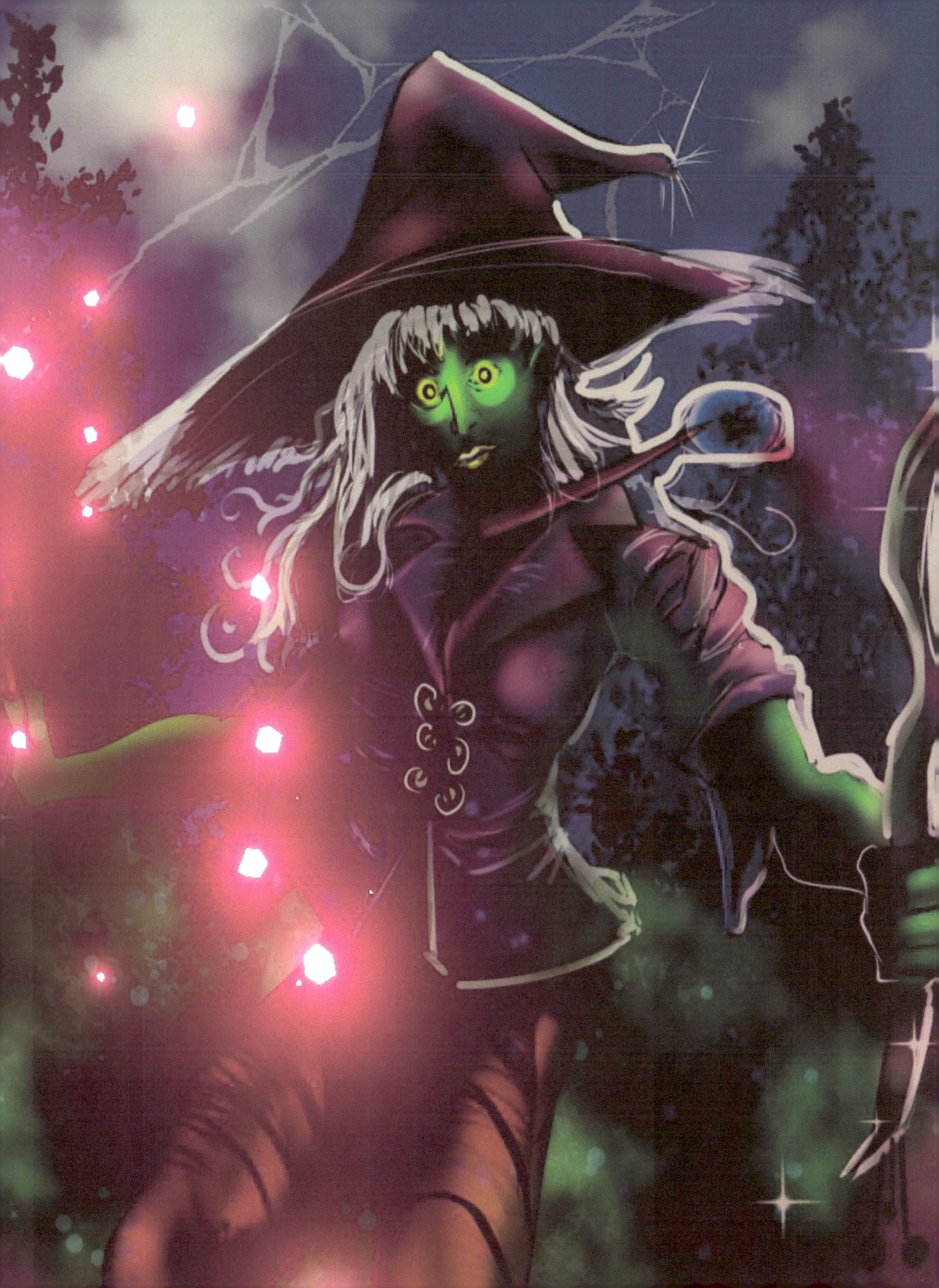

COMIC BOOK ART

The next few pages are samples of my comic book art. I like to combine stories with my art and tell short tales mostly of a ghostly nature. I have always been a horror buff. I recently completed my first horror comic called *"The Compilation of Horror"*. The first three pages are included starting with the cover on page 53.

Please enjoy!

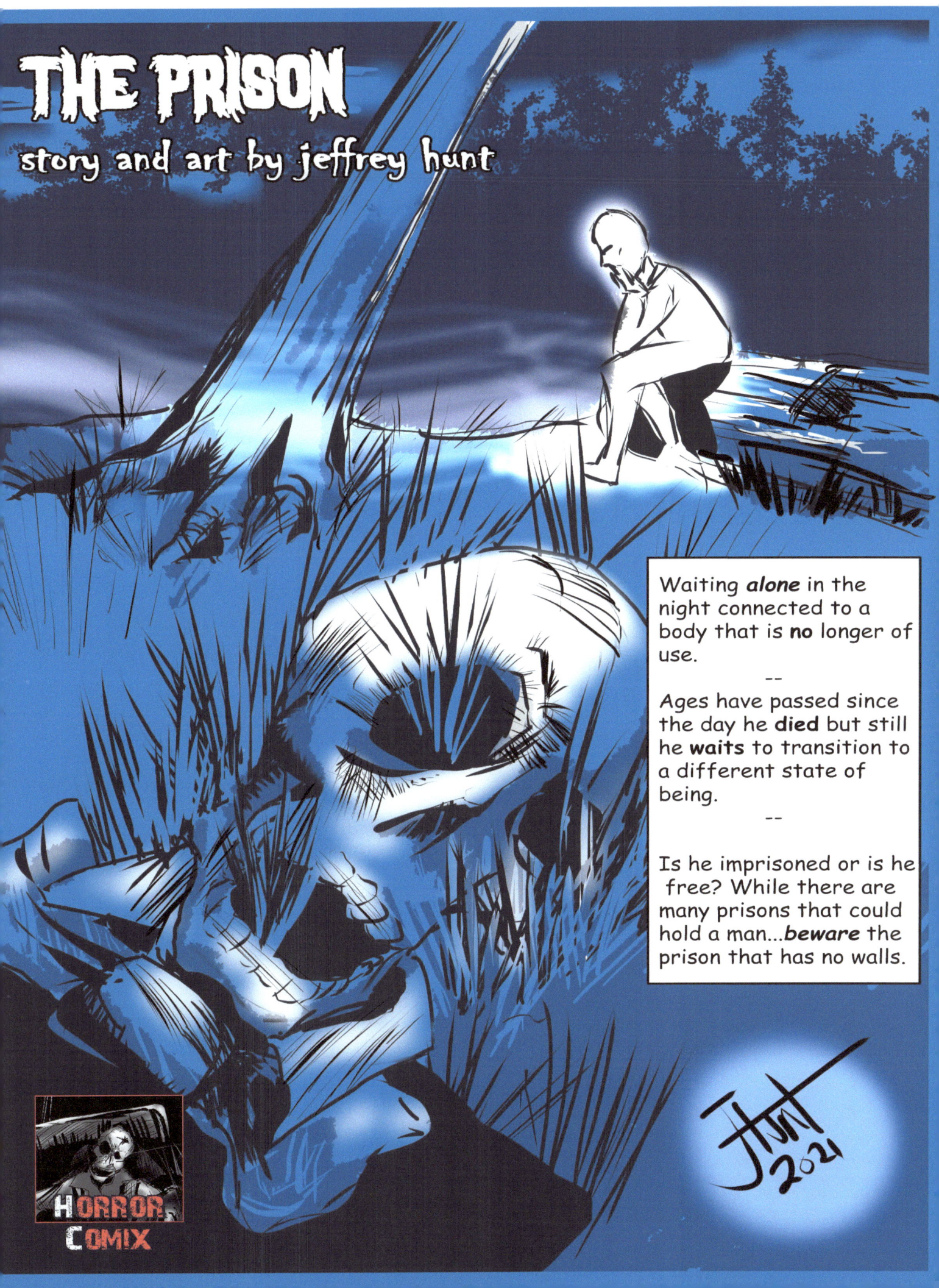

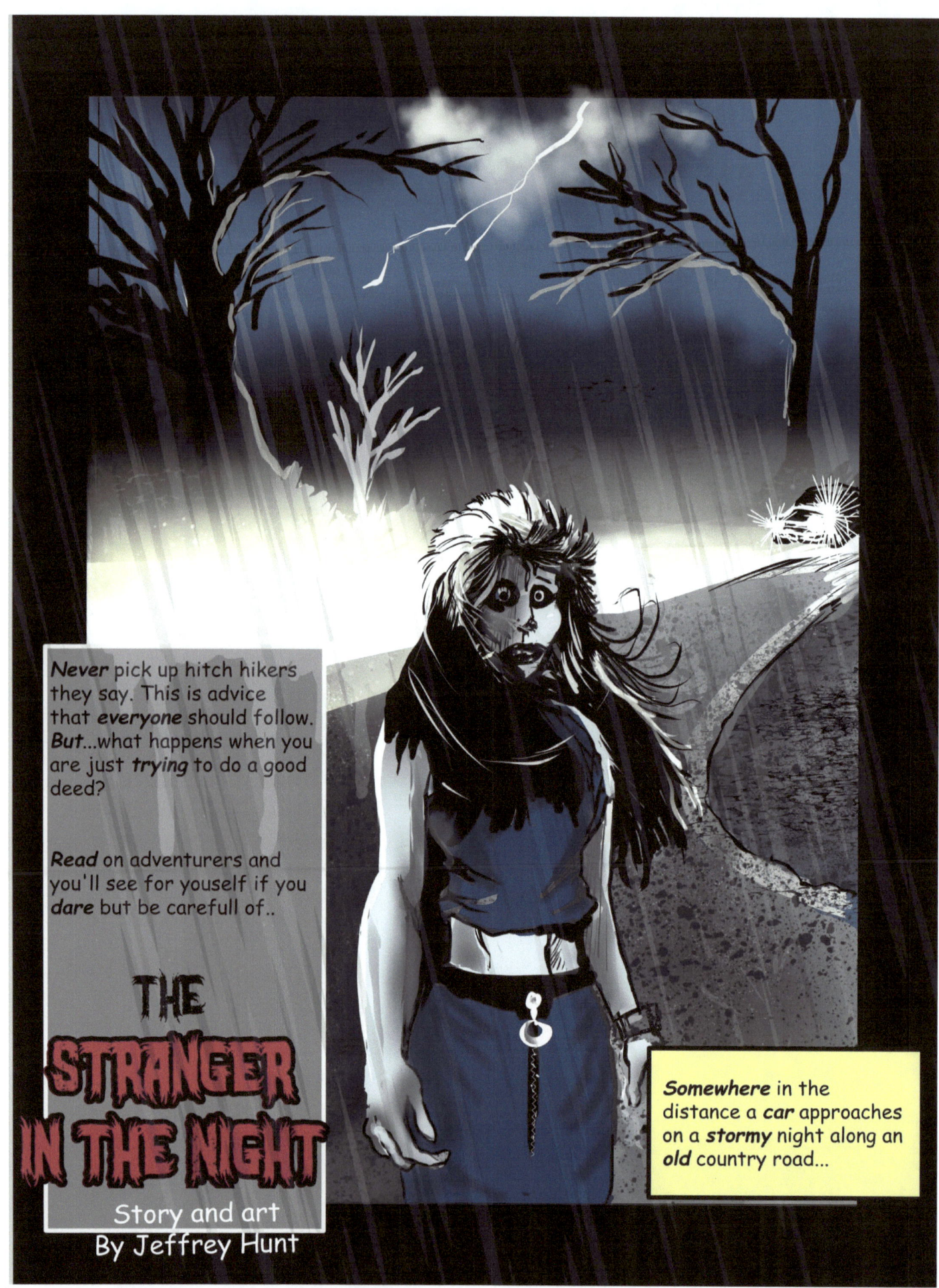

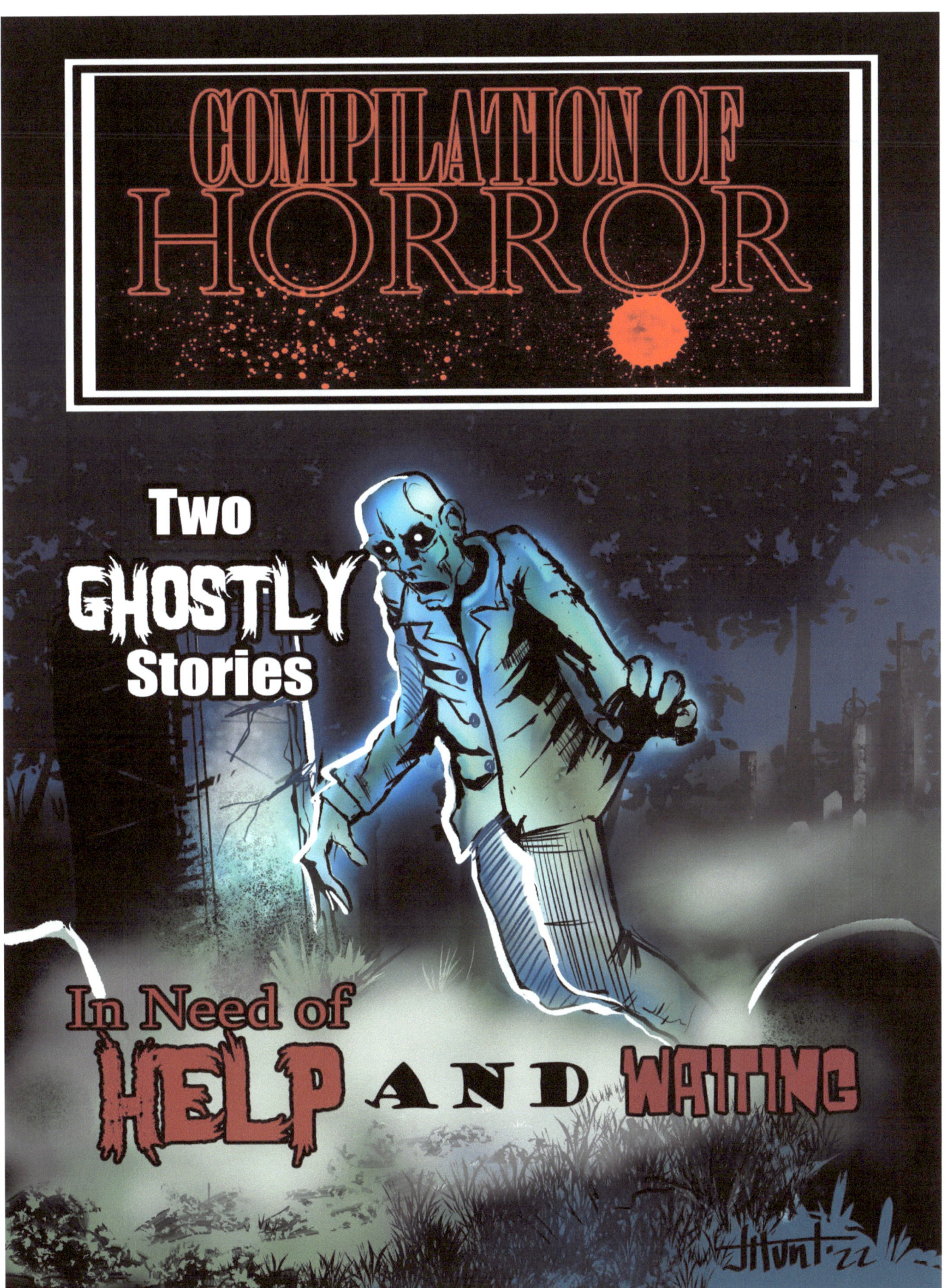

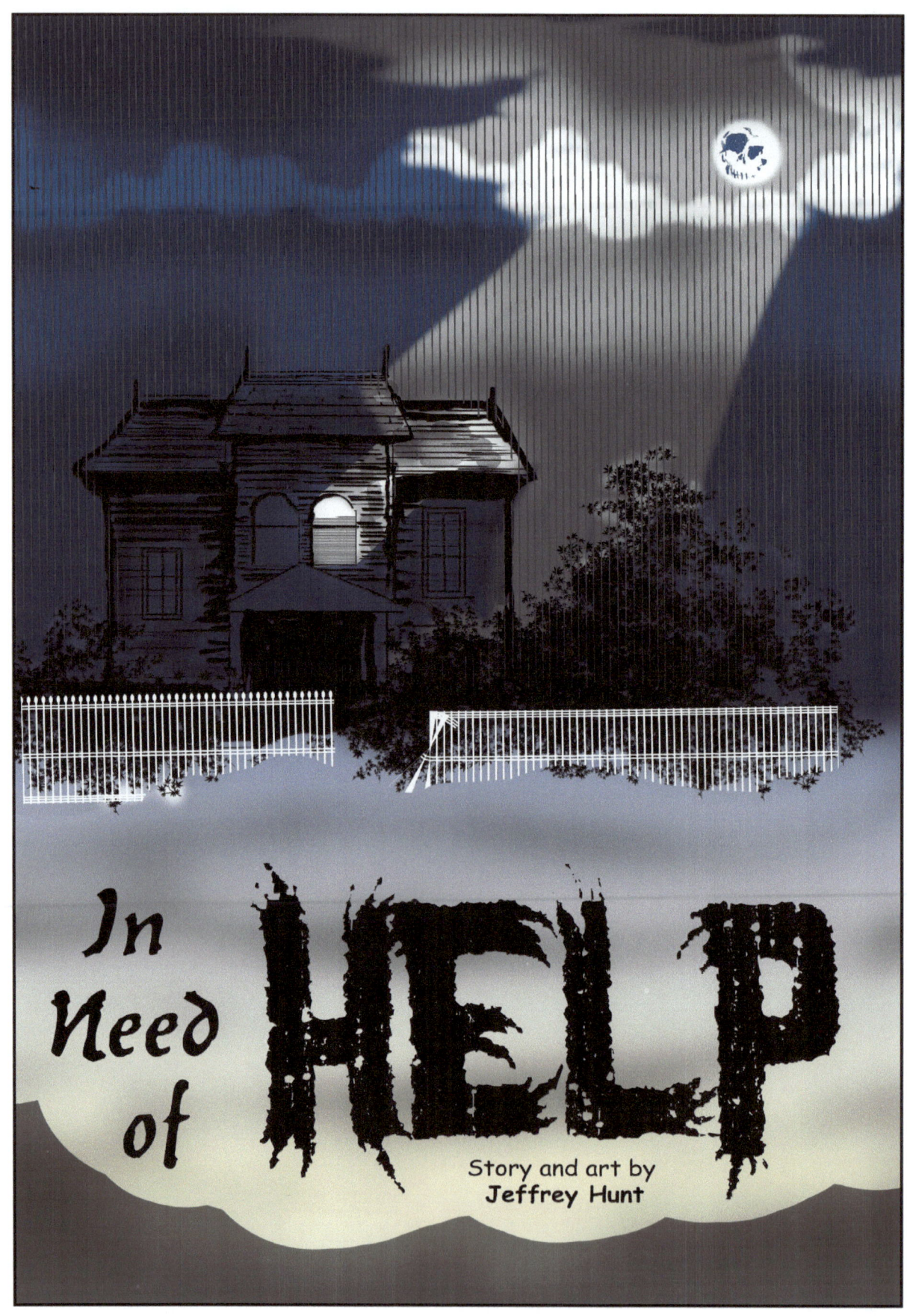

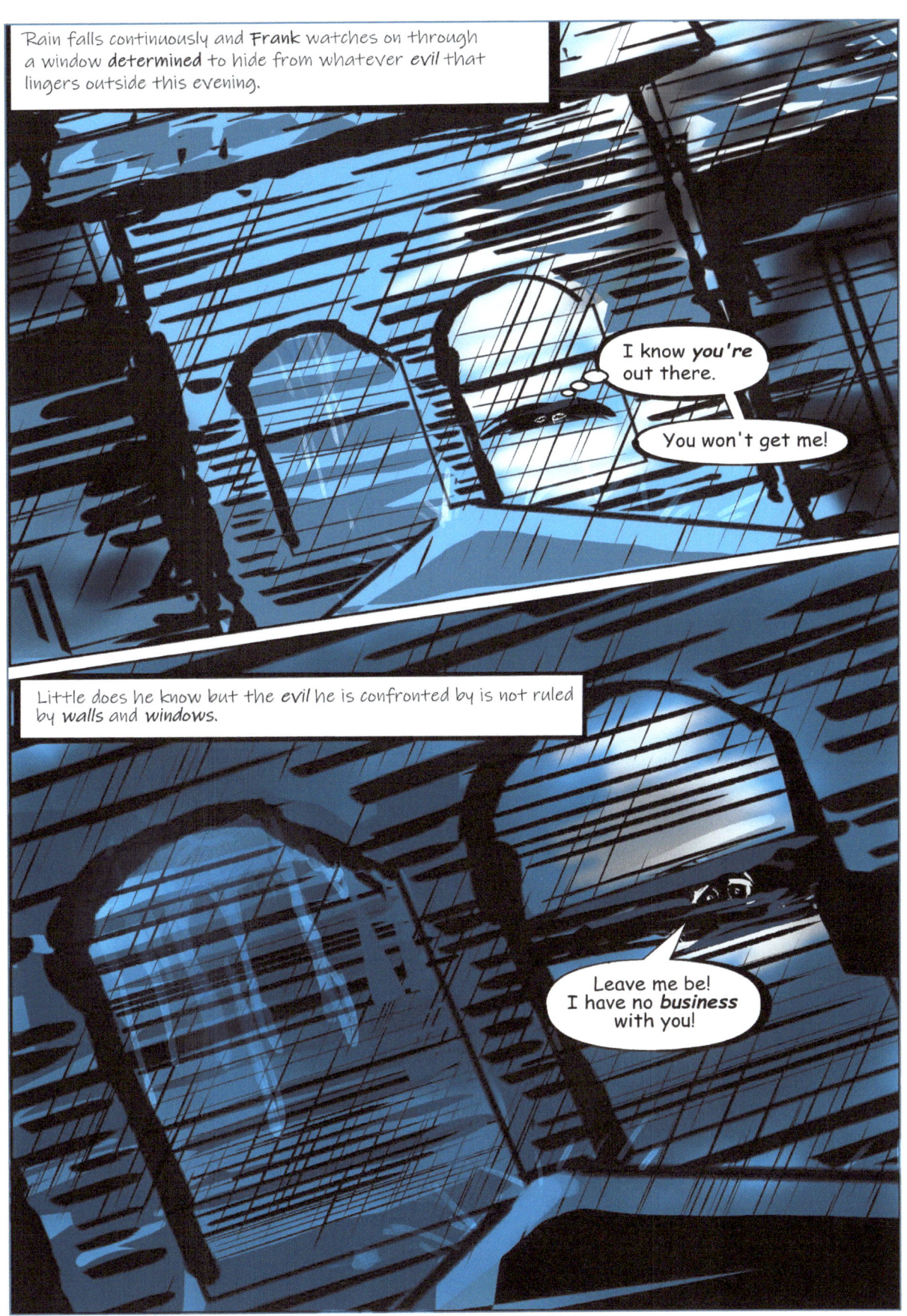

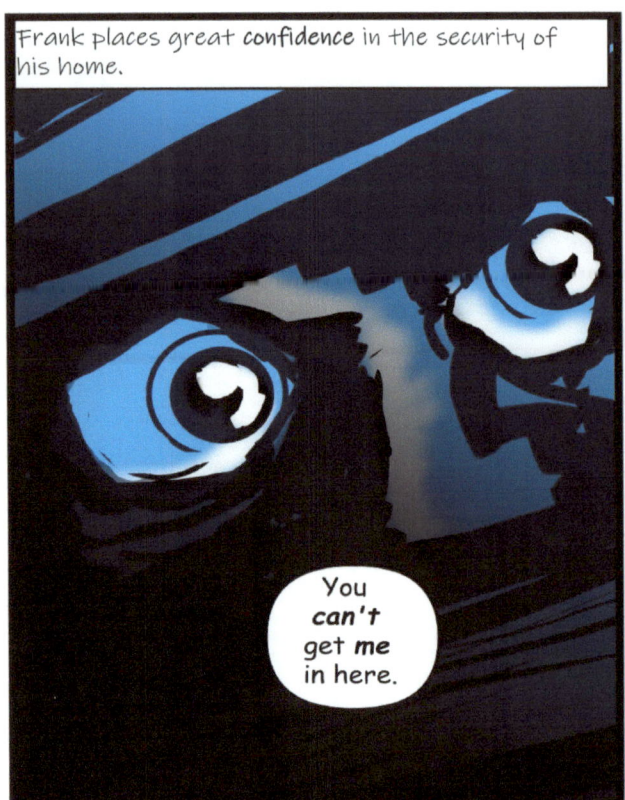
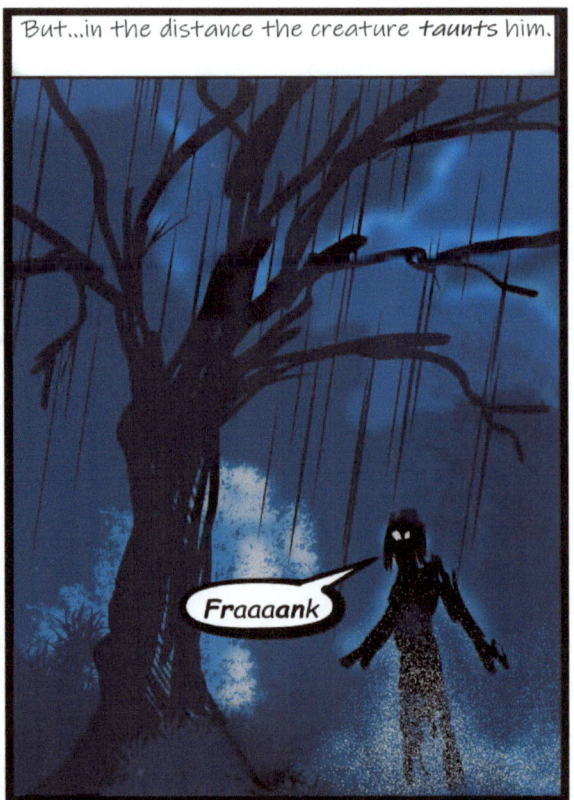
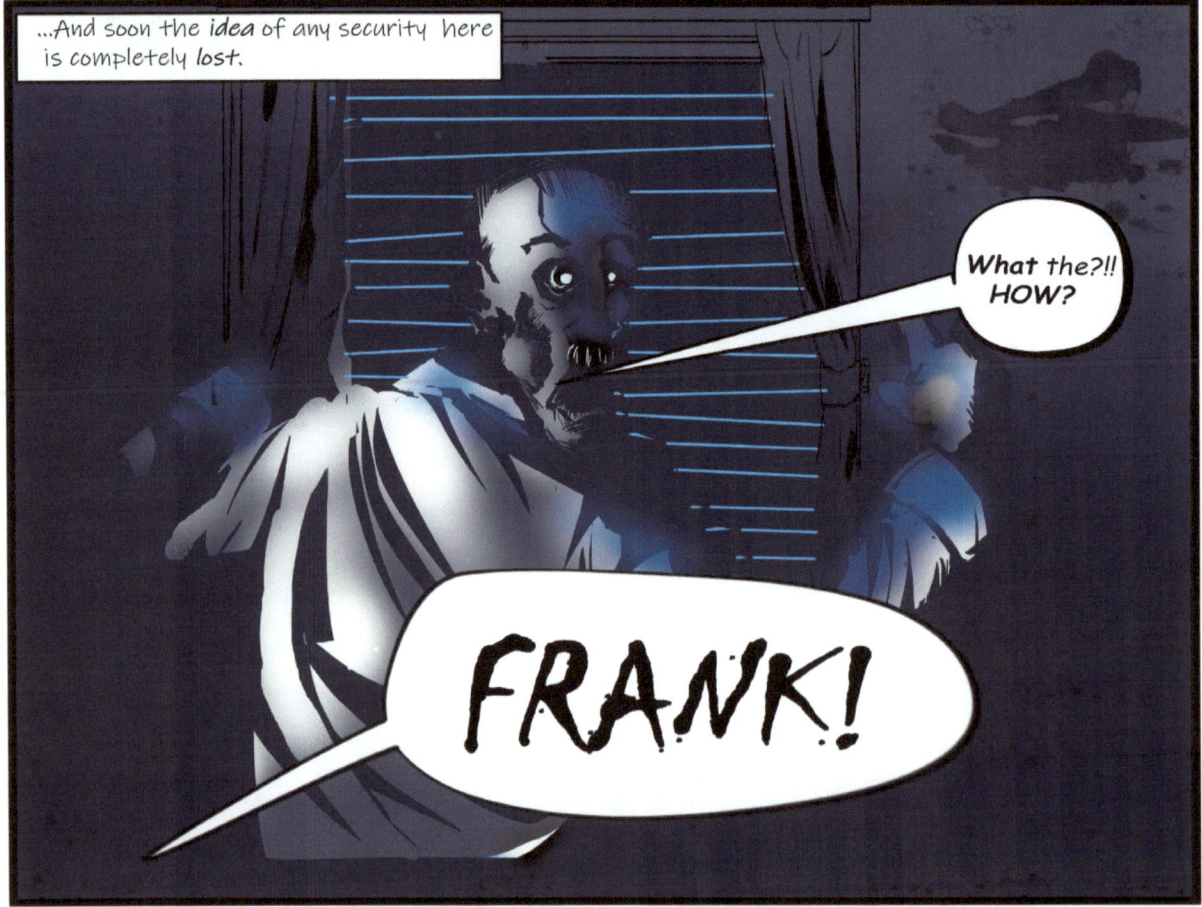

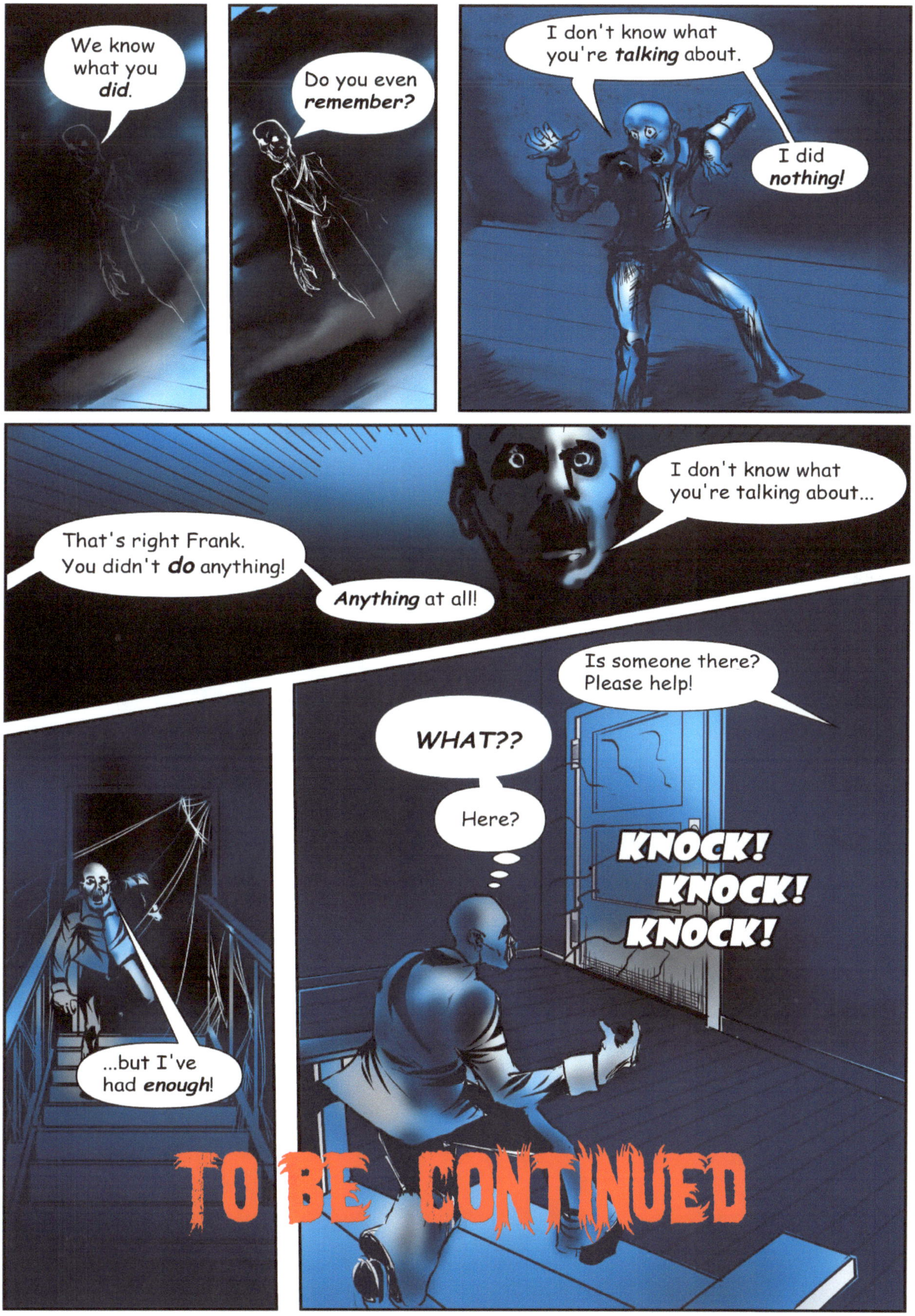

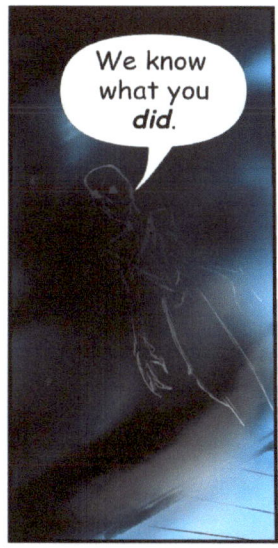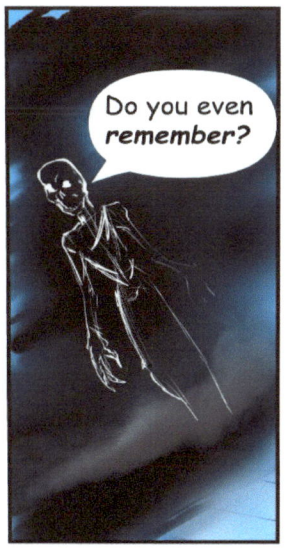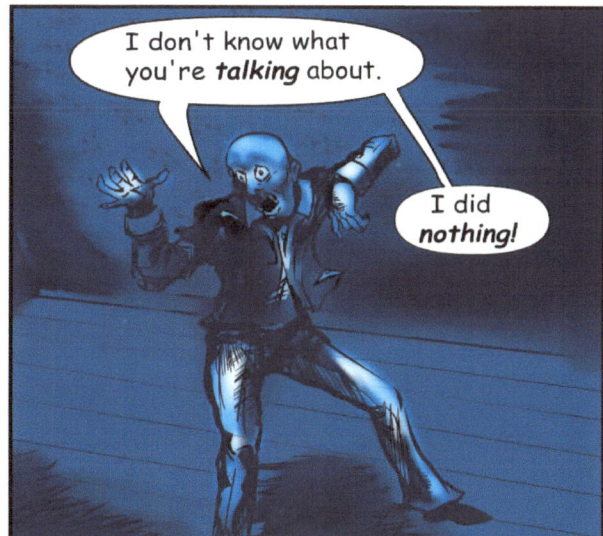

THE END

Thank you for reading my book. I hope that you enjoyed it and found inspiration and ideas for your own design work.

Also available
By Jeffrey Hunt

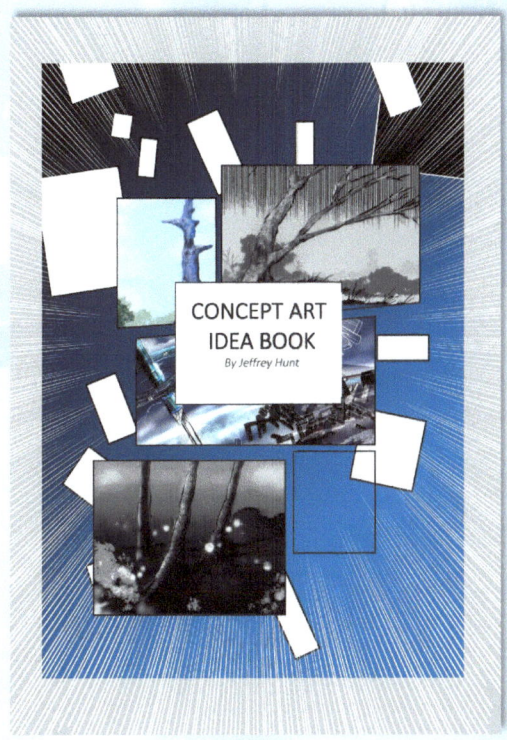

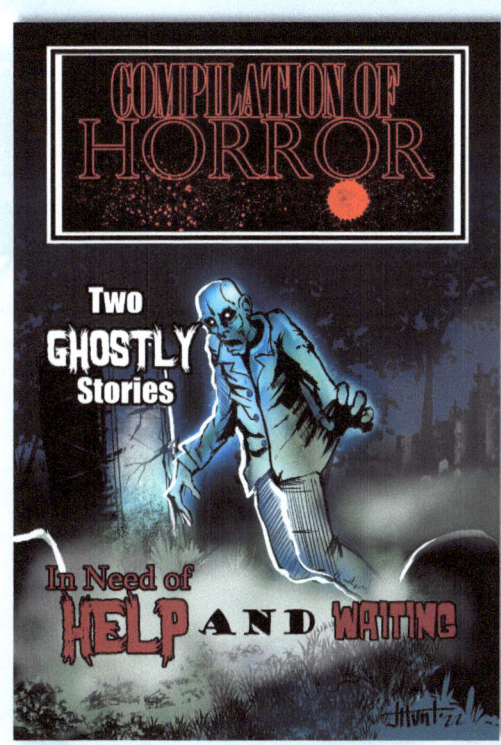

The original Concept Art Idea Book is also available on Amazon in paperback and eBook formats.

Compilation of Horror eBook is available for download at my Gumroad store.

https://jeffreyhuntart.gumroad.com/

CONCEPT ART IDEA BOOK 2

WRITTEN AND ILLUSTRATED
BY JEFFREY HUNT

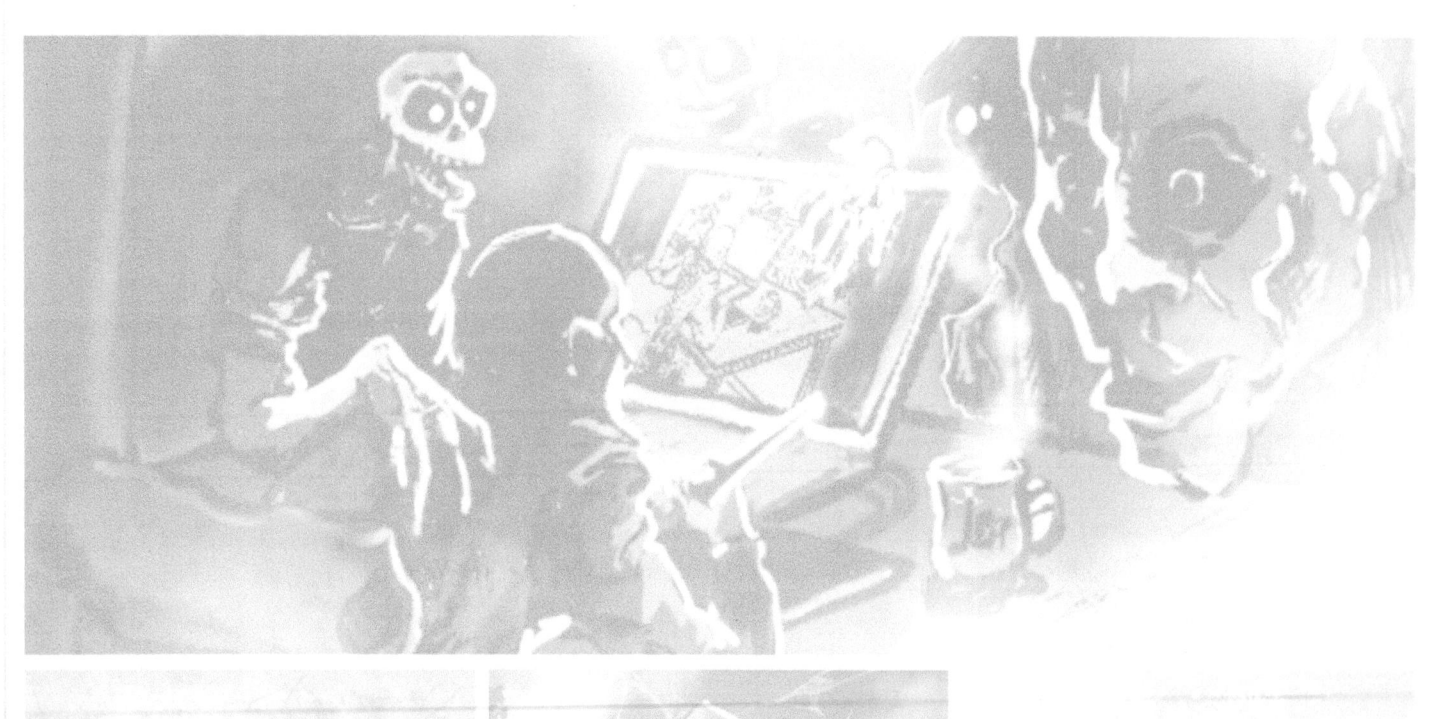

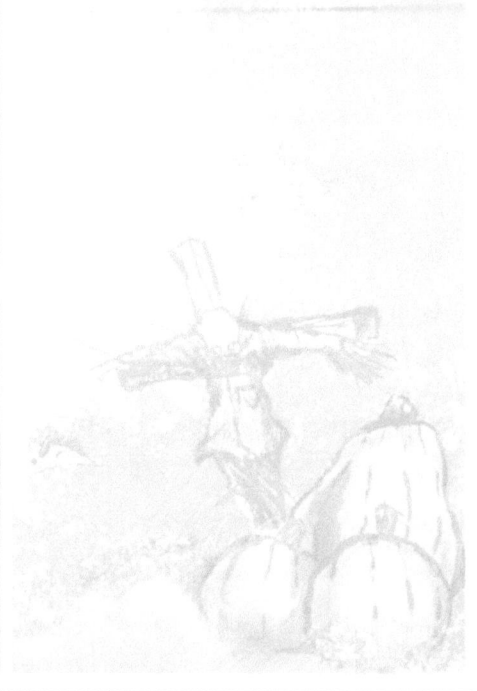

www.ingramcontent.com/pod-product-compliance
Lightning Source LLC
Chambersburg PA
CBHW051210220526
45473CB00003B/982